Stress/Unstress

Stress/Unstress

HOW YOU CAN CONTROL STRESS AT HOME AND ON THE JOB

Keith W. Sehnert, M.D.

AUGSBURG Publishing House • Minneapolis

1st printing	30,000
2nd printing	30,000
3rd printing	40,000
4th printing	35,000
5th printing	50,000
6th printing	20,000
7th printing	12,000
8th printing	15,000
9th printing	12,000

STRESS/UNSTRESS

Library of Congress Catalog Card No. 81-65647
International Standard Book No. 0-8066-1883-3

Scripture quotations unless otherwise noted are from the Revised Standard Version of the Bible, copyright 1946, 1952, and 1971 by the Division of Christian Education of the National Council of Churches.

Manufactured in the United States of America

Contents

Way No. 4:   Take Care of Your Body

Way No. 5: Provide for Your Spiritual Needs

Preface

This book, like the others I have written, is as much a chronicle of my life as a physician/author/teacher as it is a medical self-care book about stress management. It contains case histories and anecdotes gleaned from my experiences as a family doctor, father, and Christian layperson.

People who read my books often ask me, "Are the people you write about real?" When a similar question was raised once to Charles Dickens about the parade of characters found in *David Copperfield* and *Christmas Carol,* he looked the person straight in the eye and answered, "Sir, even *I* couldn't make up such characters."

The people I talk about in this book are also real. In some cases, I change their names or use initials, but in all cases the events are real. To these persons go my thanks for letting me use their stories.

I also want to thank the many authors and researchers who shared their information and advice with me about their work in stress and stress-related topics. I am particularly indebted to:

The rational self-counseling methods of Maxie C. Maultsby, Jr. at the University of Kentucky.

The pioneering work of Hans Selye at the University of Montreal.

The efforts and success of Chaplain Granger Westberg in developing the Wholistic Health Centers in Ohio and Illinois.

The work of neurosurgeon-turned-wellness-expert C. Norman Shealy in LaCrosse, Wisconsin.

The insights of psychologist Dennis T. Jaffe from Los Angeles regarding stress control through transcendental meditation and similar techniques.

John Travis and the Wellness Resource Center classes and programs he started in Mill Valley, California.

The research of Carl and Stephanie Simonton of Texas into alternative treatments of cancer.

The investigations of Herb Benson from Boston that lead to the concept of his "relaxation response."

The authors of such books as *Anatomy of an Illness* by Norman Cousins, *Mind as Healer, Mind as Slayer* by Kenneth R. Pelletier, *Ways of Health* by David Sobel, and *Alive and Well* by Arlene and Howard Eisenberg.

I am also indebted to the members of Bethlehem Church in Minneapolis who enrolled in my first stress-management classes and showed me the great interest they demonstrated in learning skills for this type of health problem.

In writing this book, the help of my wife, Colleen, was crucial, as it has been in many of my literary endeavors. As we wrote the early drafts, she painstakingly typed and critiqued those difficult first words of mine and made valuable suggestions. Writing a book with your spouse can be the real test for the strength of one's marriage. Since we're still speaking kindly to each other after this effort of nearly a year, our union of 28 years must be a good one! To Colleen, then, a special thanks.

One of my favorite poets, Emily Dickinson, once said this about the power of words:

> Some say a word is dead when it is said,
> I don't believe that's so.
> I say that only then has it begun to grow.

So, to you readers who are about to begin this book, it is my hope that its words will grow in your mind and become useful to you and the ones you love.

Part I

Understanding Stress

1

How You Can Move from Stress to Unstress

Bill Anderson is a young executive climbing his way up the corporate ladder. Forced into frequent moves as his company shifts him from one city to another, Bill feels the tension in his marriage; he and his wife don't get along as well as they used to. He also finds it hard to talk with his children. He starts to drink too much and develops ulcers.

Karen White is divorced, supporting her three-year-old son by working as a waitress. She works long hours, and is often frustrated by her customers and the management. Sometimes she takes out her frustrations on her child; then she feels guilty.

George Thompson has been an elementary teacher for twenty years—and a good one. Now he finds the children almost impossible to handle and pressures from parents and community organizations intolerable.

He has a nervous breakdown and has to take a leave of absence for a semester. He's not sure he will return to teaching.

Sarah Hunter is in her first year of college. She enjoys the freedom of being away from home but misses the familiar world of her family. College studies are much harder than she had expected. On a recent test her mind went blank and she forgot everything she had studied. She has a hard time sleeping. She wonders whether she should drop out of school.

People like this are the casualties of our age of stress. They go to make up statistics like these:

- About 25 million Americans have high blood pressure.
- One million persons have heart attacks each year.
- An estimated eight million people have stomach ulcers.
- 12 million Americans are said to be alcoholics.
- More than 230 million prescriptions are filled each year for tranquilizers.

Nearly all of us feel the stress of daily living. In a recent study (The General Mills *American Family Report 1978-79, Family Health in an Era of Stress*) 41 percent of the people surveyed said they felt a *strong* need to reduce stress in their daily lives. Another 41 percent felt *some* need to reduce stress. Only 18 percent said they felt no real need to reduce stress.

So it is normal to feel stress and to want to reduce that stress—and it is possible to do so. You can move from stress to unstress. "Unstress" is a new word for most people and suggests relaxation, peace, well-being. It was chosen to cover the concept that ordinary people like *you* can learn to handle the common problems related to stress.

Unstress is a self-care concept developed to help

handle stress. It is based on my work over the years in training thousands of persons to become "activated patients" in handling problems related to common illnesses and injuries. This work brought national attention to my Course for Activated Patients (CAP) at Georgetown University and to the medical self-care classes I have developed. The principles of the work were described in the book *How to Be Your Own Doctor—Sometimes* (Grosset & Dunlap, 1975).

All my classes were developed around three basic assumptions:

1. Ordinary people with clear, simple information can safely handle in their homes most common health problems earlier, cheaper, and sometimes better than health-care professionals.

2. Laypeople with little formal education can be trusted just as much as persons with much formal education in wisely handling such common problems.

3. Medical and nursing knowledge should not be a guarded secret of professionals but shared with the laity.

In 1970, when I started my CAP classes in northern Virginia, I steered away from advocating self-care to deal with problems of stress and related areas of emotional health. Throughout the 1960s and 1970s such problems were still "in the closet" for most people. The parents, spouses, and offspring I knew were reluctant to talk about these difficulties. It was OK to talk about *physical* illnesses but not about *psychological* ones. People found it easy to offer spontaneous outpourings of sympathy for a broken leg, but found it hard to talk to someone about a broken marriage.

Far too many of us have a flaw in our attitude about emotional symptoms. If you found your neighbor lying on the sidewalk in front of his home bleeding from cuts, you would drop everything and try to help. This same person, bleeding from emotional wounds, can be angry or hostile with you—or someone in your family—and we learn to be angry or hostile in return. A vicious cycle of hate and alienation begins.

We've also learned to get angry and hostile with ourselves, our family, friends, fellow workers, and our bosses. Sometimes this produces what people call "stress." It is more accurate to call the reaction "distress." Others will term it disillusionment, disappointment, frustration, anxiety, or just plain "being upset." What one calls it is not as important as what one does about it. By not learning other options, millions of us have resorted to tranquilizers, alcohol, or sleeping pills, which create more problems than they solve.

This brings me to the purposes of *Stress/Unstress:* to help laypersons, ordinary people like yourself, *understand stress well enough to prevent much of it in the first place.* Since we live in an imperfect world, such prevention is difficult; so that brings me to the second purpose: *learning to identify and handle stress early when it occurs.* This involves learning to listen to our body "talk" to us when we get the symptoms of emotional overload and biological signals for us to slow down, relax, get more rest, and iron out problems with other people. This, in turn, leads to the third purpose: *learning the unstress remedies* such as relaxing, stretching, exercising, massaging, listening to your favorite music, taking hot showers or baths, praying, and a whole list of other safe, self-care methods. Such remedies can be learned and used by yourself—and then taught to others you care about.

Where should you start? Begin by reading this book. Part I will help you understand stress, what it is and what it can do to you. It will analyze the common stresses that occur at home and on the job. It will show you how to determine your own level of stress and learn to recognize the danger signals that indicate too much stress.

Part II will show you how to move from stress to unstress. It will show you five ways to manage your stress, giving practical down-to-earth advice on how you can handle your stress more effectively.

Chapter 19 will help you analyze your own life and determine your Personal Action Plan for moving from stress to unstress. Chapter 20 tells you about other reading sources and places you might want to visit or contact for more information.

As you read this book, here is some advice: first, try the remedies on yourself. If they don't work the first few times, don't get impatient. Lifelong habits are often difficult to change, but God gave us minds to understand and the power and perseverance to grow and change. God also gave us the responsibility to be good stewards of all our resources, and this includes our health.

In order to maintain good health and achieve the related sense of well-being, one must have a good balance with productive work, adequate recreation, and harmony with the ones you live, work, and play with.

John Heruth noted in a Thanksgiving Day sermon at Bethlehem Church in Minneapolis, "Be it diet, exercise, creativity, work, study, health care, or whatever, we are far more productive and effective if we maintain a regular, ongoing discipline than if we develop off-and-on occasional habits . . . Students find study easier if they keep regular study habits . . . Homeowners find regular upkeep more manageable than infrequently getting things back in order . . . Runners find it possible to run a marathon if long distances are run regularly . . . Churchgoers find that regular worship brings one closer to God."

So, in the stress-management insights and tips that follow in this book, you will find agreement with Dr. Heruth that "Constant care is better than crash programs."

You are now ready to move from stress to unstress!

2

Stress and What It Can Do to You

What is stress? Dr. Sidney Lecker of the Stress-Control Center in New York said this about stress: "The word is getting beaten to death. Everybody is using it in so many different ways that stress has totally lost its meaning."

To clarify the word we turn to the man who "discovered" stress, Dr. Hans Selye, of the Institute of Experimental Medicine and Surgery at the University of Montreal. Dr. Selye, who brought the concept of stress to public attention, gives this definition: "Stress is the nonspecific response of the body to any demand made upon it."

In his book, *The Stress of Life*, Selye listed common misconceptions about stress and the correct concepts according to scientific research:

What Stress *Is*

- Stress is the wear and tear caused by life.
- Stress is a state manifested by a specific syndrome of biological events and can be both pleasant or unpleasant.
- Stress is the mobilization of the body's defenses that allow human beings to adapt to hostile or threatening events.
- Stress is dangerous when it is unduly prolonged, comes too often, or concentrates on one particular organ of the body.

What Stress *Isn't*

- Stress isn't nervous tension.
- Stress isn't the discharge of hormones from the adrenal glands.
- Stress isn't the influence of some negative occurrence.
- Stress isn't an entirely bad event.

THREE STAGES OF STRESS

In 1950 Selye published his first paper on the work he called the "General Adaptation Syndrome." His research over the years since has shown that there are three stages that follow a threatening experience:

1. The Alarm Stage. When threat is perceived through the body's senses (sight, sound, smell, touch) a message is sent to the pituitary gland in the brain where the adrenocorticotrophic hormone (ACTH) is made. ACTH then travels by the blood to stimulate the adrenals (glands attached to and over the kidneys) which manufacture adrenalin and other hormones. Their job is to cause the body to increase breathing and heart rate, raise the blood pressure, release sugars and fats into the circulation, and tense the skeletal muscles. Such actions provide the fuel and oxygen for quick energy, prepare muscles for strenuous action, help increase blood clotting mechanisms to protect against cuts or lacerations, improve the sight and hearing and other protective actions required for "fight or flight" and survival.

2. The Resistance Stage. After the immediate threat disappears, the body relaxes and returns to a normal baseline. The pulse, blood pressure, and breathing rate slow down and return to normal levels. The pupils that were enlarged to improve the range of vision become smaller. The tensed muscles of the legs and arms, ready to fight a foe or run away to a safer place, relax. The digestive system, that had ceased functioning so that extra blood could flow to the muscles and brain, resumes its normal movement and digestive functions. The bladder and kidneys, that had dramatically slowed down, now can speed up and return to their normal function—often bringing the strong urge to urinate.

3. The Exhaustion Stage. If the actual or perceived danger continues over a prolonged time, a new stage begins that can end in disease or, in certain cases, death by exhaustion. Protracted wear and tear can affect any of the body's organs or systems. In the case of the arteries in the cardiovascular system, there may be such continuous spasm that a condition develops called *hypertension* (high blood pressure). The increased blood clotting mechanisms may create a clot in a small vessel in the heart leading to a *myocardial infarction* (heart attack). Other types of wear-and-tear problems will depend on the physical and hereditary makeup of the individual. Examples include peptic or duodenal ulcers, heart rhythm abnormalities, diabetes, and nervous colon.

Each of us is the offspring of our ancestors and carry within our body the genes and the characteristics of our predecessors. These ancestors survived the vicissitudes of their times, which might have included diseases such as typhoid fever and tuberculosis, an attack by the Indians, the voyage across the North Atlantic in the hold of a crowded ship, the Franco-German War, plagues of the Dark Ages or, even further back in time, a fight with a saber-toothed tiger. With the help of a complex series of protective body actions, your ancestors resorted to "fight" (overcoming the adversary) or "flight" (running to avoid danger). Whatever the stressor, our ancestors had one thing in common: they survived, or you and I wouldn't be here!

STRESS IN DAILY LIFE

Dr. Kenneth R. Pelletier, author and clinical psychologist at the Psychosomatic Medicine Clinic, Berkeley, California, has described contemporary stress in terms of "excited" and "relaxed." Here are some case histories based on Pelletier's concept:

Case 1. "A Morning in Traffic"

1. George Blount is driving to work. He had a good night's sleep, and his body is at its baseline, or relaxed, state.
2. Just as he is about to enter the freeway, George has to swerve suddenly to avoid hitting a boy on a bicycle. Once on the freeway George has to

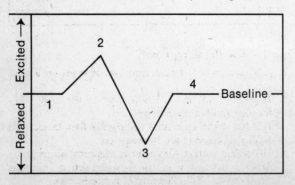

battle unusually heavy traffic because of an accident involving two trucks.

3. George leaves the freeway and drives down a quiet street near his place of employment.
4. He pulls into the parking lot and relaxes for a few minutes, talking with a friend before they start to work.

Case 2. "Just One Thing After Another"

1. Mary Ferguson has to work overtime at the office, straining to meet an important deadline.
2. Back home she learns that her teen-age son has been suspended from school.
3. Because of a loss of contracts, her husband has to take a decrease in pay.
4. Mary slips down the back steps and sustains a serious back injury.

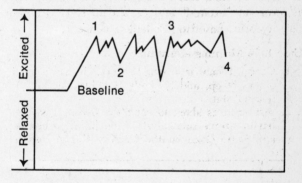

Case 3. "The Breaking Point"

1. Bill Hamilton is transferred out of town on a new job.
2. His wife finds it hard adjusting to the new community and becomes depressed.
3. Bill has a difficult time selling his first house and has to accept a much lower price.
4. His wife's mother dies after emergency surgery.
5. After a brief stay in the hospital for a "nervous breakdown," Bill is resting at home in bed.

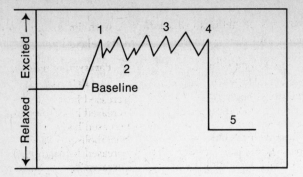

Case 4. "Spouse in Charge"

1. Dorothy Vanderkamp experiences stress after her husband returns to work and is often gone on business trips.
2. She decides to take some steps to control her stress. She begins by jogging daily to keep physically fit.
3. Their young son is injured in a bicycle accident.
4. Dorothy spends time in prayer each day and practices unstress exercises to relax her.

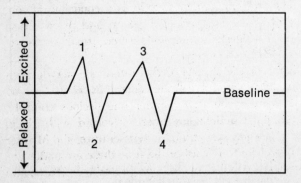

HOW YOUR BODY RESPONDS TO STRESS

In the above cases the body's remarkable autonomic nervous system is seen at work. It has two operating patterns or actions: *sympathetic*, with its excited actions, and *parasympathetic*, with its relaxed actions:

Sympathetic (Excited)	Parasympathetic (Relaxed)
Increased heart rate	Decreased heart rate
Increased blood pressure	Decreased blood pressure
Increased body metabolism	Decreased body metabolism
Increased breathing rate	Decreased breathing rate
Increased blood flow to muscles	Decreased flow to muscles
Stimulated by caffeine (coffee, tea, colas)	Decreased by exercise, sleep, relaxation methods
Stimulated by nicotine (cigarettes, cigars, pipes)	Decreased by moderate use of alcohol

The *sympathetic* pattern is the state of arousal or general alarm, when the body is put "on alert" against real or perceived danger. Individuals so aroused are ready to protect their property, livelihood, food supply, honor, or feelings.

The *parasympathetic* pattern is a condition of rest, relaxation, healing, physical repair, and regeneration. Food is digested, muscles relaxed, food stores replenished, tissues repaired.

Some of the actions of the autonomic nervous system are *voluntary* (under conscious control), and others are *involuntary* (under unconscious control). Involuntary actions are those involved with sleep, thirst, hunger, skin and body temperature, and bladder or bowel control. Most of the time these are under unconscious control, or, if you prefer, on "automatic pilot."

Unfortunately, many of us have our bodies set with the same automatic pilot as our ancestors, and it is hard for us to turn down our reactions naturally.

We learn by trial and error that a certain relaxing

hobby, special music, golfing, jogging, screaming, or crying will serve as safety valves. All too often, however, we overstimulate our sympathetic nervous system with caffeine and nicotine or overdepress it with alcohol or drug abuse—and the safety valves are not allowed to work. We allow unremitting arousal without relief and hold in our emotions. Then malfunctions occur and illness begins—with all its dire consequences.

The autonomic nervous system is controlled by complex links between the higher centers in the cortex of our brain (the "word brain") and the lower centers in the limbic or hippocampal formations (the "visceral brain"). P. D. MacLean noted in 1949:

> One of the striking observations regarding the patient with psychosomatic illness is his apparent intellectual ability to verbalize his emotional feelings.
>
> It would seem that there is little direct linkage between the visceral brain and the word brain and the emotional feelings built up in the hippocampal formation (part of the limbic systems), instead of being relayed to the intellect for evaluation, found immediate expression through autonomic centers. In other words, emotional feelings, instead of finding expression and discharge in the symbolic use of words and appropriate behavior, might be conceived as being translated into organ language.

In Case 1, "A Morning in Traffic," the sympathetics for fight or flight are activated in 2. The parasympathetics started in 3 and a baseline state is achieved in 4.

In Case 2, "Just One Thing After Another," the sympathetics are being constantly stimulated in 1, 2, 3, and 4, and the parasympathetic balance is not experienced at anytime except while sleeping.

In Case 3, "The Breaking Point," the sympathetics

are in constant state of overdrive, and relaxation is not achieved until the situation is so severe that hospitalization is required.

In Case 4, "Spouse in Charge," there is a good balance obtained between sympathetics and parasympathetics by learned use of meditation, prayer, and unstress exercises.

Research has shown us that biological stress patterns, unless controlled, frequently lead to disease. The graphs of such patterns in the case histories shown illustrate what can happen. There are great differences in the stress tolerances of individuals, and the tolerance can be exceeded in anyone—and therein lies the challenge of increasing understanding of stress, its causes and prevention.

STRESS CAN BE GOOD

Dr. Selye has emphasized that stress is not always bad for you. How you perceive a particular event is determined by your attitudes. An event can be experienced as pleasant (positive stress), unpleasant (negative stress), or as neutral. Selye coined words to cover this range of experience. Negative stress he called *distress,* defined as suffering or a state of danger. It is what most people commonly mean when they say someone is stressed. Positive stress he labeled *eustress.* He chose the Greek prefix for *good,* also found in words like *euphoric* (good feelings) or *euphonic* (good sounds).

"Adopting the right attitude can convert a negative stress into a positive one—what I call eustress," Dr. Selye said. "For example, I doubt if anyone, even a person with a naturally high stress threshold, could endure my busy schedule unless he took as favorable a view of my work as I do. In either case, the stress,

The Two Stress Reactions:
Distress and Eustress

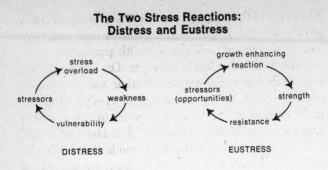

the schedule, is the same, but for me it has become eustress. Being the descendant of several generations of dedicated physicians, I was told as I grew up that hard work is both an obligation and, if approached by the right spirit, a pleasure, and I certainly have found this to be true.

"I think the cultivation of this attitude toward life was also responsible for helping me in several ways. 'Imitate the sundial's ways, count only the pleasant days', was a folk proverb I often heard while growing up in Austria-Hungary, and it made a deep impression on me. I find I've learned to quickly forget unpleasant incidents and that I cannot carry grudges for very long. If wronged by some friend or colleague, as happens to almost everyone in some point in life, I may break off contact with the person out of sheer self-protection, but I bear him little enmity. After all, Nature gives even the most fortunate of us only a limited capital of energy to resist stress, and it would be silly to squander it on quite pointless anger or hatred."

DR. SELYE'S SECRET RECIPE

I have had the pleasure of visiting Dr. Selye several times. I particularly remember a long visit I had with him in Columbia, Maryland, in 1977. A group of other physicians and I, plus several nurses and scientists, had spent the day discussing health promotion methods and medical self-care concepts. Dr. Lorenz L. Ng, one of the sponsors of the meeting and a research scientist at the National Institute of Health at nearby Bethesda, asked the famous scientist to summarize a lengthy paper he had presented that afternoon.

Selye, smiling a grandfatherly smile, turned to Ng and said, "Larry, what you really want me to do is to distill the importance of thirty years of work on stress in three minutes. OK, here is my secret recipe for the stresses of life.

"The first ingredient is to test your own limits, decide if you're a race horse or a turtle. Then structure your life accordingly. Don't fool yourself.

"The second step is to choose your life's goals. Test them to see if they are really yours and not some forced on you by an overly helpful parent or teacher. If you really want to be a scientist or a surgeon, make sure it's your *choice*. I've seen too many cases of doctors who wanted to be musicians and accountants who wanted to be carpenters. That only causes suffering as these folks try to live out choices others made for them.

"The third and perhaps most important ingredient in the recipe is altruistic egotism—looking out for oneself by being necessary to others and earning their good will. Help others, and you will help yourself. Practice altruistic egotism. Make your deposit in their Bank of Good Will."

Selye commented further about altruistic egotism the next day in his lectures. He warned that altruism and egotism must be placed together in moderation. There can be danger in extremes. Extreme altruism, constantly putting other people's interests before your own, is as dangerous to your health as the pursuit of ruthless egotism, "looking out for Number One." He noted that there is as much tragedy in the parents who put their children above themselves and become self-suffering shells as there is in the individuals who, having clawed their way to the top, created so much ill will that there is no one left to share the view from the top when it is finally achieved.

Professor Selye pointed out that one cause of much of the spiritual malady present today in epidemic proportions is the loss of altruistic goals. He deplored the notion, made popular in certain bestsellers, that you can live entirely for yourself without giving much thought to others.

In my last meeting with Selye, one of the physicians in the group said to him, "Your concept of helping others so that you will help yourself sounds a lot like the Golden Rule or the Christian way of life."

Selye, concluded, "It sure is. It also represents the wisdom of the ages, and it is the secret seasoning in my recipe!"

3

The Family Under Stress

Family life is a major source of stress today. To see evidence of this stress, you have only to pick up your local newspaper and scan the pages. One particularly gruesome article appeared in the *Minneapolis Tribune:*

SON APPARENTLY KILLS PARENTS WHO PAID HIS BAIL

A Brooklyn Park man whose parents mortgaged part of their farm to bail him out of jail apparently killed his parents and himself at the farm Monday or Tuesday. He was to have been sentenced Wednesday to receive psychiatric treatment.

The story went on to tell how the man's parents had raised $15,000 by mortgaging their Blue Earth County, Minnesota, farm after their son had been jailed. Although the 33-year-old man had no history of emotional disturbances in the past, investigators recommended psychiatric treatment because he was despondent since his wife left him and refused to return. That story had all the far too common elements we read about in our newspapers and see on television: divorce, separation, suicide, murder, alienation—dramatic examples of the American family under stress.

CAUSES OF FAMILY STRESS

A few statistics highlight the changes in family life in America that are causing increasing stress:

- Nearly half of all marriages end in divorce.
- 40% of all children born in this decade will spend part of their youth in homes with only one parent.
- Households headed by women have doubled in the last 20 years.
- Only 16% of today's families fit the traditional concept of mother, father, and children, with Dad the breadwinner and Mom staying home to care for the family.
- The number of unmarried couples living together has more than doubled since 1960.
- The average homeowner stays in a single home for about seven years.
- 20% of all families in America move each year.

What has caused these changes in family structure? Is it the mobility of Americans, women's lib and changing family roles, permissiveness in child training, our jobs, the failure of the schools, weakened church life? Has there been a destruction of the moral values that have sustained humankind throughout its history? Let's examine some of the possible causes:

In commenting on the mobility of modern families, Alvin Toffler says in *Future Shock:* "The magnitude of moving 36 million Americans from city to city is the same as if the combined populations of Cambodia,

Ghana, Guatemala, Honduras, Iraq, Israel, Mongolia, Nicaragua, and Tunisia were to be forced from their homes and be relocated. That news would make front page headlines, but the huge migration within America seems to go without much flourish!"

Average Americans may move because they are switching jobs every three years. That often brings about traumatic changes in habits, social ties, and schooling. An official in IBM's medical department observed that such changes involve losses of some kind: "Familiar faces, places, pleasures, ways of doing things and organizational supports are changed . . . such losses are more severe than many persons recognize."

Another significant cause is that of changing family roles. In less than one generation, the traditional roles played by men and women have undergone greater change than they had in the last ten generations. One marriage counselor observed:

> After awhile you begin to sense that their real problem is that they feel lost, confused and alienated because the roles of being a husband or a wife or a parent have changed so much from the day when they were kids. They no longer know what the standards and values of family life are today. They don't know what to tell their kids.

One significant role change brought about, in part, by the women's liberation movement, has been that of women switching from homemaker to breadwinner. Economists predict that by the late 1980s more than half of the labor force in America could be women, including half of all mothers with school-age children. Increasing numbers of women taking professional positions in the business world will have an enormous impact on corporations and the communities of people around them. Males will be dealing with female bosses, and women will be reevaluating themselves as peers—and bosses. For many situations there will be few precedents and few role models to study.

Eli Ginzberg, a health economist and professor at Columbia University, has observed that the changing roles of men and women is a worldwide phenomenon and not limited to the United States. He calls the role change the "single most outstanding phenomenon of this century."

The economic and social changes that have resulted have opened up a Pandora's box of problems. One human relations expert noted: "Everybody's in favor of equal pay, but nobody's in favor of doing the dishes!"

The changing nature of our work has also caused problems. Opportunities for work and the size of corporations and companies significantly affect the kind of jobs Americans have. Companies are getting bigger and bigger. For example, one of the major legal actions of present times was the decision of the U.S. Supreme Court to split Standard Oil Company into 11 separate companies: Standard was considered "too big." Now, 70 years later, Peter Drucker pointed out, *each* of the separated companies are larger than the former company was in the early 1900s.

When the United States became a nation in 1776, about 75% of its people earned their living on the farm or were closely involved with agriculture. The large family was the rule, and cooperative work by its members was essential for survival.

A hundred years later, as America was about to enter the twentieth century, the majority of Americans still worked on farms or in small family-owned businesses. Now as we approach the twenty-first century, less than 3% of people work on farms, and the small family-owned enterprise is the exception rather than the rule. Today more than 50% of the American labor force work for major national and regional corporations. Rewards for services and producing products are becoming complex. Individuals now surround their endeavors with titles, job descriptions, responsibilities, departments, divisions, and organizations. Changes in jobs occur at an alarming rate. Loyalty to company as well as family, church, and community are eroding. The multiple transitions that are required and changes that go with them have created stress for all concerned.

Another cause for family stress has been the erosion of traditions. A transformation has occurred in the games its children play, the education of its youngsters, the courtship of young adults, the jobs, the role of the church, and the religious traditions of families.

Observers who look at the discouraging fragmentation of the family, note that not all the changes have been for the worse. The life of the average person is unquestionably easier than that of our ancestors. Life in the old days was harsh and often even brutal. Life spans were shorter. Improvements in transportation, household appliances, entertainment, medical care, and education have, without doubt, made life in the 20th century much better.

Ironically, however, some of these improvements designed to enhance our quality of life, have simultaneously impaired our health and that of our families. Our automobiles with their high speed bring us 50,000 deaths and several hundred thousand serious injuries each year. Our refrigerators and home freezers allow us to own a family delicatessen with rich, high caloric foods that provide 24-hour nibbling and raise havoc with our body weight. The omnipresent TV set, a boon for entertainment, becomes a bane which produces an increasingly sedentary life and decreased family conversation and personal interaction.

Our modern society has lost many of the supports, traditions, and convictions that have helped people endure hardship and suffering. The work to keep us fit, the sense of place in our community, the religious faith that helped America become great and allowed its citizens to survive with peace of mind have all diminished in recent years.

OUR TOWN, U.S.A.

The story of family life in one small town in Pennsylvania dramatizes the changes that have occurred across the United States:

Roseto was founded by several Italian families in 1883. When they moved to northeastern Pennsylvania, the men found work in the quarries along the Delaware River. As stone masons, the men lived a life similar to the males they had known before, and the women maintained the homes and raised their families as they had in the old country.

The people lived in tightly knit Roman Catholic families, and their children learned traditional values. They might have been able to continue their quiet, hard-working lives had they not reached Modern Times, achieved prosperity, and been singled out as a town where no citizen under 47 years of age had a heart attack!

Roseto became famous in 1961 as the "Miracle Town" because, despite eating traditions that featured meals amply supplied with high-cholesterol cheese and fatty meats, and citizens who tended to be on the plump side, the incidence of heart attacks was only one-third the national average.

By 1971 when medical researchers returned to study its citizens, some dramatic things had occurred. Modern Times had descended on the city. Men no longer worked in the slate quarries but commuted to work at out-of-town jobs. Families had enough money to join country clubs in the nearby Poconos and get into a new social whirl. TV antennas rose from every roof. New homes were being built everywhere. The sale of Cadillacs was up.

But on the other side of the coin, many of the women had gone to work at nearby factories to help foot the new bills. Church attendance at Our Lady of Mt. Carmel dropped. Divorce and family problems had increased dramatically.

Researchers found something else about the city and its citizens: as Roseto's problems became more widespread, its incidence of heart attacks climbed back to the national average!

Is the lesson we learn from this that over-involvement with oneself, at the expense of community and church, can lead to psychological dislocation? America's families both in Roseto and elsewhere are troubled and stressed. Through ignorance and neglect, members are falling ill unnecessarily. Some, because they do not heed the signals and stress warnings their body is sending them. Others, because they don't realize that lay people, with training and Christian concern, can learn to handle many common problems.

4

Stress on the Job

If family life is one of the major stress areas in our lives, our jobs are another.

A recent study by the National Institute for Occupational Safety and Health has provided valuable insight into just who is experiencing stress on the job. It's not, as you might expect, the high-powered executive pictured in movies and soap operas. It's not the harassed surgeon pictured in the TV series, *General Hospital*.

Here, according to this study, are the 30 most stressful jobs:

1. Health technicians
2. Waiters, waitresses
3. Licensed practical nurses
4. Quality-control inspectors
5. Musicians
6. Public relations
7. Laboratory technicians
8. Dishwashers
9. Warehouse workers

10. Nurses' aides	20. Health aides
11. Laborers	21. Taxi drivers
12. Dental assistants	22. Chemists
13. Teachers' aides	23. Bank tellers
14. Research workers	24. Social workers
15. Computer programmers	25. Roofers, slaters
16. Photographers	26. Secretaries
17. Telephone operators	27. Registered nurses
18. Hairdressers	28. Machinists
19. Painters, sculptors	29. Bakers
	30. Metal workers

There are critics of this study. They point out that the research was based on data obtained at state-financed mental health centers in Tennessee. It may have excluded people with higher incomes, such as professionals and business executives, more likely to seek private care than public treatment. Nevertheless, the two-year study provided valuable insight into on-the-job stress.

If you weren't a "Stress Bowl Finalist," then how did you rank? Are you a physician (ranked 106 on the stress list), a reporter/editor (46), policeman (70), or a bus driver (91)? If your day was particularly hard, what can you learn about stress from these more stressed people? What things do the Top Thirty have in common? What do Betty, the waitress at the Tasty Inn, and Ben, the orderly at Midwest Hospital, have to face on their jobs that your boss at the plant or your surgeon doesn't have to contend with?

CAUSES OF ON-THE-JOB STRESS

1. **No control of working situation.** Betty has little or no control of her working situation. When her customers want prompt, speedy service, she has to contend with a temperamental cook, a new water boy, a busy cashier/hostess, and the woman who makes the

salads. She is often "shot down" by the restaurant's inefficient system.

Although Ben's order was to get the elderly patient from his bed to the x-ray room, the orderly has to contend with a slow elevator and even slower operator, two student nurses, one resident physician, and a cranky x-ray technician, to say nothing of the frightened patient and his worried family. Ben took 20 minutes for a trip scheduled to be completed in half that time.

2. Low pay scale. Both Betty and Ben look at their jobs as simply a way to earn money to support themselves and others. Betty is divorced and supporting her five-year-old son. Ben is a former pre-med student working as an orderly since he dropped out of college. He is not married and is living at home with his mother and disabled father. He wishes he were back in school. Although many other individuals at the restaurant and the hospital may look at their work as an opportunity for self-expression and achievement, Ben and Betty find little personal or financial fulfillment from their jobs.

3. Limited job training or guidelines. Because the work requirements for both jobs are limited, Betty's and Ben's managers assume that little job training is needed. Responsibilities were poorly defined and briefly described on the first day of work. From then on, it's on-the-job training. For inexperienced employees this can create a lot of anxiety—and it did for both our waitress and our orderly. When that was coupled with indifferent supervisors, the old maxim, "A happy employee is a productive employee" took a 180° turn for the new employees at the Tasty Inn and Midwest Hospital.

Undoubtedly, the greatest stress factor for Ben and Betty was their *lack of control* over their jobs. This has been confirmed in many studies over the years. Four of the better known include:

1. **The Swedish train study.** Scientists in Sweden were able to measure the amount of a stress-related hormone, epinephrine, in the urine of volunteers who took the commuter train to Stockholm. Group One got on the train at the first stop, 79 minutes from the city, while Group Two got on the train midway, 43 minutes away from their destination. Although both groups agreed that the ride got increasingly stressful as they approached Stockholm, those commuters who got on the train *first* actually secreted *less* epinephrine. Those who boarded the train first felt a greater freedom of choice. They could choose their preferred seat, find plenty of room for coats and briefcases, and even sit with their friends. The key factor was *control*. Those who boarded midway had to scramble for seats, sit with strangers, and adapt themselves to situations in which they had little control. The result for them was a more stressful ride in to work each day, and they gave chemical proof of it in their urine samples.

2. **The California freeway study.** Scientists at a California university attached pulse monitors to the wrists of executives who were instructed to keep a diary of their activities each day. The diary was then correlated with the record of their pulse rates. When the data were analyzed, the scientists found that the highest pulse rates were found in the volunteers who drove on the freeways. The process of dodging cars, fighting traffic jams, and watching for unexpected stop lights presented situations with one thing in common: these drivers felt they *lacked control*.

3. **The O'Hare air traffic control study.** This study involved a review of the medical records of the 94 controllers and trainees at Chicago's O'Hare Airport. It showed that only two had worked there for more

than 10 years. The records also showed that two-thirds of the employees had ulcers or symptoms of ulcers; more than 35 controllers had been removed for psychiatric reasons since 1970, and the incidence of high blood pressure was four times as frequent as that found in pilots checked by Federal Flight Administration medical examiners. The reason for such findings was the feeling by these employees that they not only had to make split-second decisions that affected the lives of hundreds of passengers each day, but they often felt they were *not in control* because of many factors such as weather, pilot error, and equipment failures.

4. The DuPont Company study. A three-year study at E. I. duPont de Nemours and Company showed that initial heart attacks after the age of 45 were more frequent among lowest salaried male employees than among those in the highest pay brackets. In fact, the men in the highest brackets had the lowest rate of heart attacks. Researchers concluded that the higher the job position, the more satisfaction the executives derived from the challenges of their work and the less stress they reported. Executives felt less stress because they received assistance from secretaries and administrative aides. Executives had *more control* of their work than employees in lower levels, who felt frustrated by limitations in their work environment.

HOW YOUR PERSONALITY AFFECTS JOB STRESS

We have seen that *lack of control* is a major cause of stress on the job. A second major factor is your personality.

Two San Francisco doctors, Meyer Friedman and Ray Rosenman, did a ten-year study in which they learned that a certain type of personality was three times more likely to get heart attacks. They reported their findings on these stress-prone individuals in a book entitled *Type A Behavior and Your Heart.*

The doctors, both heart specialists, found it was not just the number of cigarettes these persons smoked, or their cholesterol level, or even their blood pressure that determined who got the coronary, it was their attitude and temperament. Were these candidates for coronaries the high men on the totem poles? No, not necessarily, although many were, but many others didn't make it to the top. They pushed their self-destruct button along the way!

The results obtained by Friedman and Rosenman were similar to those observed by Dr. Flanders Dunbar in the 1940s in studies at New York City's Columbia Presbyterian Medical Center. She attempted to match up personality traits with various medical problems. Among the heart-attack patients she observed were many highly trained professionals and businessmen who seemed to have difficulty sharing responsibilities with others. The more trying life became, the unhappier these patients were. The unhappier they became, the harder they worked. Dunbar made this observation about these patients: "They would rather die than fail."

What characteristics do these Type A people have?

1. **Tendency to overplan.** By overplanning the day's schedule, these individuals become victims of a chronic sense of time urgency. Their schedules become so tight that the slightest setback quickly becomes a major disaster.

2. **Multiple thoughts and actions.** These people are

habitually involved in more than one thought and action at the same time. It is not unusual to see them eating a meal—while reading the paper and listening to the radio—*and* carrying on a conversation. Their speech patterns are rapid, and they habitually interrupt the conversation of others. Their "conversations with others" are usually monologues. It is apparently impossible for them to listen to others for more than a few seconds.

3. Need to win. Such stress-prone persons have to win if they are to be happy with themselves. They become agitated and unhappy if they don't win at even trivial business or social activities.

4. Desire for recognition. The Type A personality has a persistent desire for recognition that can pervade everything else they do. They are also overconcerned with earning money and collecting material things as proof of their success.

5. Always feeling guilty. These persons, who can't relax without feeling guilty, tend to overschedule and overplan leisure and social activities to the point where even their social life becomes burdensome. Leisure time designed for reducing tension instead becomes for them a way to produce it.

6. Impatient with delays or interruptions. Stress-prone people have little patience with others whom they may perceive as doing a task too slowly. Whether or not they have the responsibility to oversee the "slower person's" work, they may interrupt them to show a faster method or watch with obvious exasperation.

7. Overextend themselves. The strong desire for achievement and recognition forces them to be overextended in multiple projects and activities. In doing so, their creativity and judgment may be jeopardized.

8. Sense of time urgency. These individuals have a continuous struggle against time. Because they overplan, they constantly feel frustrated by all that has yet to be done in order to meet their overly ambitious goals.

9. Excessive competitive drive. Although competition is an integral part of American life, the stress-prone person usually goes beyond normal limits. They view everything as a challenge, and if they don't win are restless and discontent.

10. Workaholics. These individuals are the people who pride themselves at being the first at the office in the morning and the last out at night. They have no time for recreation, exercise, family, or friends. Such disturbances in relationships can be destructive for all concerned.

ARE YOU A TYPE A?

Now for the moment of truth. The Self-Test on pages 46-47 will help you determine whether you are a Type A personality, and therefore whether you face a high risk of cardiac illness or other stress-related diseases.

SELF-TEST FOR "TYPE A" PERSONALITY

As you can see, each scale below is composed of a pair of adjectives or phrases separated by a series of horizontal lines. Each pair has been chosen to represent two kinds of contrasting behavior. Each of us belongs somewhere along the line between the two extremes. Since most of us are neither the most competitive nor the least competitive person we know, put a check mark where you think you belong between the two extremes.

	1	2	3	4	5	6	7	
1. Doesn't mind leaving things temporarily unfinished		X						Must get things finished once started
2. Calm and unhurried about appointments				X				Never late for appointments
3. Not competitive					X			Highly competitive
4. Listens well, lets others finish speaking					X			Anticipates others in conversation (nods, interrupts, finishes sentences for the other)
5. Never in a hurry, even when pressured						X		Always in a hurry
6. Able to wait calmly					X			Uneasy when waiting
7. Easygoing					X			Always going full speed ahead
8. Takes one thing at a time					X			Tries to do more than one thing at a time, thinks about what to do next

	1	2	3	4	5	6	7	
9. Slow and deliberate in speech	—	—	—	—	—	X	—	Vigorous and forceful in speech (uses a lot of gestures)
10. Concerned with satisfying himself, not others	—	X	—	—	—	—	—	Wants recognition by others for a job well done
11. Slow doing things	—	—	—	X	—	—	—	Fast doing things (eating, walking, etc.)
12. Easygoing	—	—	—	X	—	—	—	Hard driving
13. Expresses feelings openly	—	—	X	—	—	—	—	Holds feelings in
14. Has a large number of interests	—	—	X	—	—	—	—	Few interests outside work
15. Satisfied with job	—	—	X	—	—	—	—	Ambitious, wants quick advancement on job
16. Never sets own deadlines	—	—	—	—	X	—	—	Often sets own deadlines
17. Feels limited responsibility	—	—	—	—	X	—	—	Always feels responsible
18. Never judges things in terms of numbers	—	—	—	—	X	—	—	Often judges performance in terms of numbers (how many, how much)
19. Casual about work	—	—	—	X	—	—	—	Takes work very seriously (works weekends, brings work home)
20. Not very precise	—	—	X	—	—	—	—	Very precise (careful about detail)

SCORING: Assign a value from 1 to 7 for each score. Total them up. (Turn to the next page for analysis of your score.)

ANALYSIS OF YOUR SCORE

Total score=110-140: Type A₁.

If you are in this category, and especially if you are over 40 and smoke, you are likely to have a high risk of developing cardiac illness.

Total score=80-109: Type A₂.

You are in the direction of being cardiac prone, but your risk is not as high as the A₁. You should, nevertheless, pay careful attention to the advice given to all Type A's.

Total score=60-79: Type AB.

You are an admixture of A and B patterns. This is a healthier pattern than either A₁ or A₂, but you have the potential for slipping into A behavior and you should recognize this.

Total score=30-59: Type B₂.

Your behavior is on the less-cardiac-prone end of the spectrum. You are generally relaxed and cope adequately with stress.

Total score=0-29: Type B₁.

You tend to the extreme of non-cardiac traits. Your behavior expresses few of the reactions associated with cardiac disease.

This test will give you some idea of where you stand in the discussion of Type A behavior that follows. The higher your score, the more cardiac prone you tend to be. Remember, though, even B persons occasionally slip into A behavior, and any of these patterns can change over time.

Credit: Dr. Howard I. Glazer, director of behavior management systems at EHE Stresscontrol Systems, Inc.

In the description of the range of scores, the most extreme "Type A" personality is the Type A₁, the hard driving, overly conscientious person. At the far end is

B_1, the "laid-back," extremely easygoing person. Most of us, of course, are somewhere in between.

After you've analyzed your Self-Test for Type A personality, you might be better able to answer a question I've heard in the business world, "Who's more stressed, the boss or the errand boy?" The boss with a score below 60 when compared to an errand boy who scores 80 or 100 is less stressed despite their obvious differences in pay, responsibility, etc.

The important thing, however, is how *you* scored. But even if you have a score that made an A_1 or A_2, don't be *distressed*. Part II of this book will give you practical tips to help you control stress on the job and at home.

5

From Stress to Professional Burnout

In the previous chapter we looked at stress as it relates, in general, to our jobs. In this chapter we will look at the problem of professional burnout, especially of people engaged in special kinds of jobs—the helping professions—like doctors and nurses, clergy, and teachers.

DOCTORS AND NURSES BURNOUT

The early warning signals regarding professional burnout may have been apparent to some observers for a long time, but they didn't know what to label the problem.

In the area I know most about, the health professionals, perhaps it wasn't so much that we didn't know what to label the problem as that *we were afraid to acknowledge it existed*. Perhaps there was even a conspiracy of silence. After all, aren't we supposed to be the helpers, who provide the support for others in need?

John-Henry Pfifferling, Ph.D., of the Center for Well-Being of Health Professionals in Chapel Hill, North Carolina, recently stated, "Every year this country loses the equivalent of seven entire medical school classes to doctors' suicides, drug addiction, and alcoholism alone. Most people working in the field would agree that about 10 percent of all physicians are seriously impaired, meaning that their patients receive inferior care. Serious impairment includes: alcoholism, drug abuse, major depression, other severe psychiatric and emotional disorders, serious marital and family problems, and so on. It does not include all lesser levels of impairment: chronic burnout, controlled alcoholism, chronic unhappiness, alienation, depression, and personal disorganization—any of which can adversely affect patient care."

He also noted, "American medicine is at once a mirror for American society and an example of the work ethic carried to extremes. . . . The problem for physicians often begins with medical training programs run with an underlying philosophy that trainees should overwork and if a trainee cannot take the stress then he/she should get out of the kitchen. . . . Traditionally considered smarter, more dedicated, and harder working than their peers in other occupations, physicians run a higher risk of developing serious disabilities."

The case history of Dr. Leo Stone (not his real name) provides a clear example of the serious disability he developed from alcoholism:

Leo graduated No. 1 in his medical school and got a top surgical residency in the East. Later he joined the U.S. Navy Medical Corps and served there for 10 years. Stone had just left the service when I met him at a county medical society meeting. He told me, "I plan to build the biggest surgical practice in northern Virginia."

Stone rented an expensive office, bought a big house in Fairfax County and before long was rumored to be earning over $100,000 a year. I saw him periodically at the county medical society meetings, and it seemed that it was "all systems go for Leo"—at least for a while. When we visited, he bragged about his long hours and many patients.

I didn't hear much from Leo for a couple of years, and then I heard he had separated from his wife, had been picked up for driving while intoxicated, and was moving to Arizona.

Something serious had happened to Leo. As his stress increased, his abuse of alcohol increased in a vain effort to soothe his emotional hurting. He became an alcoholic, but refused to acknowledge his problem or seek help.

Later I was able to piece together these six key elements of the impaired physician in Stone's story:

1. **Community involvement.** Although at one time very interested in community affairs, as his alcohol dependence increased, Leo withdrew from community, professional, and social activities. We never saw him at the medical society meetings, at church, or the country club.

2. **Family life stress.** There was strife in his family. He was often abusive to his wife. His teen-age sons, once good students, were especially affected, and both ended up with all sorts of problems in school. As alienation with his wife increased, Leo started running around with an airline stewardess 20 years younger than himself. Soon thereafter, Stone and his wife separated.

3. **Employment changes.** After three or four years of rumored office problems, Leo left his surgical part-

ner, had several interim offices, and finally decided to move to Phoenix. The alcoholic physician sought to run away from his personal and professional problems. This is called taking the "geographic cure."

4. Physical status. Stone's physical appearance changed. Formerly a rather dapper dresser, he let his hair grow long and had an unkempt look about him. A former close friend told me he looked "terrible."

5. Office conduct. His office nurse reported to a mutual friend that Leo had lengthy absences from his office and jumbled his appointments. His patients reported he was often angry and hostile with them, a common characteristic of the alcoholic.

6. Hospital conduct. The last thing we heard before he moved to Arizona was that he made so many mistakes in his orders that the nurses reported him to their supervisors. He often made his rounds at midnight or in the early hours to avoid seeing other physicians on the staff.

Dr. Stone, once a winner, became a loser through alcoholism. He neglected his own well-being at great expense to himself, his family, and his patients. The fruits of Leo's harried life and overachieving were personal, financial, and physical collapse: professional burnout.

Doctors are the product of a long and complex medical education program during which they are trained to believe that they should appear to be all-knowing. And nurses, since the days of Florence Nightingale, have been expected to do an emotional balancing act that involves long hours, low pay, demanding patients, and unswerving dedication to their calling in the face of the frustrations associated with the bureaucracy of hospitals. Aren't they supposed to be able to provide time and hand-holding and brow-wiping for dying people and their troubled families without needing to recharge their own emotional batteries?

Many nurses I know, especially those involved in the high-technology world of intensive care units and operating rooms, feel that they have little control over their work world. When you add too many long nights, appalling injuries from automobile and motorcycle accidents, and executives with failing hearts, the New Age Nightingales come to a point when they have simply seen—and felt—too much. Burnout then occurs.

Burnout has been defined as a state of physical or psychological exhaustion that is related to chronic, unrelieved pressures. Mitzi Duxbury of the University of Minnesota School of Nursing said, "It's a very pervasive problem in the helping professions. Nursing is basically the use of your therapeutic self, and these are the kinds of people who tend to burn out quickly."

Jan Lee was one of the "statistics" described by Polly Kirby from Big Sur, California, when she said, "About half of all nurses who complete their training end up quitting." Jan served on the second shift of a hospital in St. Paul. She told me about the night she had simply seen—and felt—too much.

Before that night, a nagging sense of hopelessness had been working on her for several weeks. Jan felt the frustration, but she still did her job as conscientiously as she could. Then one night it happened. Jan recalled the details: "I had just come on duty when a badly injured, middle-aged farmer was wheeled into my ward. He had been brought in by ambulance from a small town near the Twin Cities. There had been an accident with a corn picker. His arms were both gone and a vertebra was crushed in his upper spine. He was paralyzed from the chest down."

Jan remembered the moment that the patient slowly

came to his senses. He gasped for breath on the respirator attached to his nose and tried to speak, but no sounds came. Eventually she could read his lips. She knew what he was saying. "How long—how long will I be like this?"

Jan said she doesn't remember how she answered him or what happened during the rest of that long night when she worked over him and talked to his children who had come to the hospital.

"It was a night full of tears. All their emotions caught up with me by the end of the shift, and I started to cry. I was unable to finish my work," Jan said as she looked back. "That night I decided to leave my job and have decided not to return to nursing."

CLERGY BURNOUT

The clergy can face a similar problem. Tim Martin (not his real name) was ordained in 1968 and for ten years served two small-town churches. He said, "I was plugging along at 16-18 hours per day, teaching in high school during the week and then on call at night for family problems and as needed for weddings and funerals. I worked nearly every weekend. I was under the gun seven days a week."

Tim said he didn't notice the pressure until 1973 when one of his parishioners—who had become closest of his friends—died. "After that," Tim went on, "everytime the phone rang, I jumped. I had trouble preaching and seemed tired all the time. I ended up in the hospital with pneumonia.

"Apparently I had lapses of memory. People who knew me said I looked tired, had sunken cheeks, and looked pale. I eventually took the summer off and went back to college for six weeks—to recover.

"I began to consider leaving the ministry in 1976

when I started getting depressed, tired all over again, and unable to cope with people's problems. I took a one-year leave of absence in 1977, but I knew I'd never return. I just couldn't bear it anymore. As I look back on it now, I was becoming burned out."

I asked Tim, "Now, as you look back, what would you say happened and how might you have maintained more control of your life as a pastor?"

Tim sat back, rubbed his chin for a minute and said, "It would be difficult, but I've thought about that many times since I resigned. What I'd like to do before I accepted a call would be to get everyone in the church to a meeting and tell them something about me. I'd tell them this:

- You have to take me as I am. Don't put me on a pedestal. I don't want you to think I have all the answers.
- You are to call me Tim and not Pastor Martin. When I'm out socially, I'd expect to pay my own way. No special favors. I don't want to be thought of as better than the lay people in the church.
- I want to be active physically. If I feel like baling hay or doing other hard work, I'd like to do it without being criticized.
- I want one or two days off each week to pursue other outside activities, and I'd want to share the church with another pastor for on-call situations that come up.

"Maybe I'd insist on a contract. I would also take better care of my health. I'd get more sleep and have better eating habits. I'd take more vacations to keep my attitudes fresh."

As Tim looked at his watch and told me he had to leave soon, I asked a final and hard question, "Was it just *you*? Were you not cut out to be a pastor?"

Tim looked me straight in the eye when he gave me his answer, "No, it wasn't just me. I knew many students as they entered the seminary. They were a neat bunch—emotionally well-balanced, intelligent, ready to serve. Over the next 10 years I saw these same men. They were overeating, overdrinking. They had become sad and lonely people. They were simply worn out.

"As to whether or not I should have become a pastor," he continued, "most of the people said I was a good pastor. When others heard I was considering leaving the ministry, some replied that if only I had enough faith, I could stay in."

"Blame the victim?" I said.

"Yes, sort of, but I have no remorse," said the former clergyman. "I'm happy in my new career as a counselor. I'm staying fit by chopping wood and biking. I've limited my work to 40 hours per week. I don't even think of myself much anymore as an ex-pastor. I like to tell my friends that 'I retired early.'"

As I left the interview and drove home, I felt sad about what had happened to that dedicated pastor and a system that can "chew up" its clergy and "spit" them out and not know why. On the other hand, I felt happy because Tim had survived a most difficult personal dilemma and had come out of it with his sense of humor still intact. Maybe his experience would not only help other ex-pastors, but help bring reforms in the way we treat our clergy.

TEACHERS CAN BURN OUT TOO

"Burnout is most observable in jobs that require heavy people contact," says Beverly Ferguson of Metropolitan State University in Minneapolis. "Teachers are experiencing job burnout in ever-increasing numbers."

When I drive past the elementary school where

Paul Nelson teaches, the building doesn't look dramatic. In fact, it looks downright peaceful. It apparently was peaceful when Paul started teaching there over a decade ago, but times have changed. Now when he comes home, his wife Sally tells me, he often sits down at dinner with such severe headaches that he can't eat. Some days he gets so drained and tired that he calls in sick. Paul said, "If it weren't for our place up north where we go to recover each summer, I'd quit, especially after last year."

Paul ticked off the frustration of teaching these days, while Sally, a former teacher herself, nodded in agreement: increased discipline problems, budget cuts, larger class sizes, more unhappy children from families split by divorce, newly arrived students from around the world with various ethnic backgrounds who speak English with difficulty.

Today's schools are also filled with students who spend five hours per day watching TV and find the real classroom less entertaining than the version they see at home on shows such as *Welcome Back Kotter* and *Sesame Street*.

Sally said, "Today's teacher is expected to correct most of society's problems." Paul retorted, "You can say that again!" as he related how he had to break up a playground fight last spring. One of the fighters bit him so deeply in the arm that Paul had to go to a local emergency room for treatment. During the process of breaking up the fight, Paul slammed the big sixth-grader against the fence. Within a few hours the boy's divorced father stormed into school with the complaint, "You assaulted my son, and I'm going to sue you!"

"I have lost control of the classroom," Paul said. "The administrators didn't back me up in that lawsuit. I can't even keep a kid after school unless I keep a log on an unruly student for a long time. There's no immediate action I can take for a disruptive student. The class sizes grow larger—and stay large—because of budget limitations. The mix and makeup of students become more difficult each year."

Sally chimed in, "Although teaching is becoming a *Catch-22* situation, there are some answers: (1) make smaller class sizes; (2) let teachers have authority to remove disruptive students; (3) give classroom teachers adequate support for special education problems and non-English speaking students; (4) quit threatening teachers every year with loss of jobs and budget cuts for books and supplies; (5) make administrators stop implying that teachers who stay in the classroom are failures because if they were 'any good' they would have become principals."

Both Paul and Sally suggested there is an even more complex answer to the teaching problems: there should be fewer working mothers. According to them, most of the children in school these days are unsettled and lack discipline. They have been farmed out much of their lives—nursery school, preschool, day-care centers. The mothers—and fathers, too—justify this by saying: "We're giving our child *every opportunity possible*."

I noted that I had heard similar statements and often felt it was a socially acceptable statement that hid more complex problems, such as fear of parenting, role confusion, and family priorities that put the emphasis on financial security over emotional and spiritual security.

Sally agreed with me and said this about such parents, "They really don't know what to do with Johnnie and hope someone else does. No wonder the kids are bored with school and confused!"

EARLY WARNINGS

What early warnings did Tim and Jan have that might have tipped them off about their impending burnout? What might Paul be experiencing now? Some telltale sentences I picked up in my interviews included these:

"I'd get up and dread going to work."
"I was irritable and I didn't like myself. I worked all the time."
"I was in a rat race."
"At no time did I feel in control of my job."
"I wasn't certain any more of how objective—or even competent—I was in my work."
"I couldn't muster enough enthusiasm to care."
"How much could one person put up with?"

These were the early warnings of disillusionment, depression, alienation, disorganization, and unhappiness. Fortunately, none of the three people I talked with became seriously impaired or developed complications such as alcoholism, drug abuse, psychiatric and emotional disorders, or marital and family problems. Jan, Tim, and Paul recognized their problems—both internal and external—and took actions before some of the more destructive complications arose. Leo waited too long.

The next two chapters will help you learn to recognize the signals that indicate that stress is reaching the critical stage of burnout.

6

How Much Stress Is OK?

Hans Selye, the father of stress research, has theorized that over a lifetime, each of us seems to have a certain amount of adaptive energy to cope with our environment. Thus, if individuals have to respond to several illnesses, many life changes, a difficult marriage, and a life so filled with difficulties that their bodies are in a state of chronic arousal—from real or perceived psychological threats—they will wear out sooner. Such persons will be old before their time. Sometimes an event, even though it could be relatively mild, will be "the last straw," and a serious illness could result.

Selye has further theorized that each individual must learn to conserve this adaptive energy before it is depleted. In many ways such attitudes about conservation are like those regarding our nation's reserves of oil, gas, and electricity. Just as Americans can no longer drive gas-guzzlers and waste electrical energy, we as persons can't "burn all our lights and appliances" without the danger of running out of adaptive energy.

When the body has depleted its energy and the person feels completely exhausted, these things happen: the muscles no longer function as well or get cramps; the mind doesn't function smoothly; the emotional state is changeable, and one cries easily or can get hysterical—all signs that the human motor is sputtering and getting ready to stall. This is an example of too great a load, too much wear and tear.

On the other hand, we all have seen people who have too little stress: the unemployed carpenter sitting around all day bored and out of sorts; the prisoner in his cell staring dully out the window; the formerly active fastidious housewife, now a widow, inactive and unkempt, adjusting to life in a retirement village. All are examples of underload and too little stress.

The Forbes Continuum (see Chapter 7) is a concept used by managers in manufacturing and business operations. It shows the need to balance stimulation, responsibility, and challenge in work assignments. The close link between stress and productivity is one reason why a great deal of research has been conducted by people in the business world.

HOW CRITICAL EVENTS CAUSE STRESS

Research has also been done to determine how critical events in a person's life affect the physical and mental health of an individual. Initial research at Johns Hopkins University under Adolph Meyer in the 1930s and then further expanded in the 1950s and

'60s at the University of Washington's School of Medicine by Thomas Holmes and Richard Rahe was done on significant life events such as marriage, death, and divorce and their impact on people. It eventually led to the Social Readjustment Rating Scale.

Over a period of 20 years Holmes and Rahe conducted more than 5000 interviews to try and link major life-events with illness or injury. The interview probed events—those perceived by the people they interviewed as being positive, such as job promotions, vacations, marriages—and as negative, death of a spouse, divorce, change of residence. The research staff then gave 43 critical events numerical ranking from 0 to 100.

One major positive event, marriage, turned up more often in the interviews than anything else and weighed more heavily than most, so it was given an arbitrary value of 50. That placed it halfway up the scale.

The researchers then started looking at stress and asked 400 men and women—from all religious persuasions and walks of life—to compare marriage with the other 42 events which had been identified from the interviews. They asked the people to assign numerical values to events that required more readjustment than marriage, or less. Time for social change, comparative severity to the family involved, and personal distress were considered and ranked. Out of these comparisons came the Life Change Unit (LCU).

The data uncovered in this major study were used in a wide variety of settings and audiences and seemed generally applicable to people regardless of race or age. Minority groups in the United States, such as blacks and Latinos, assigned much the same point values as white Anglo-Saxons.

Ongoing studies have shown that an individual who

scores 150 or fewer LCUs in a year is considered in the normal range and is not likely to have been stressed enough to risk illness or injury in subsequent months. Those who score 150-199 had enough stress so that 37% of them had an appreciable health problem. People who scored between 200 and 299 reported that 50% experienced some sort of illness or injury within the ensuing year. Those that had so much crisis in their lives that their score was above 300 were found to have illness or injury in 80% of the cases. Of the individuals that scored 350 to 400 points, 90% reported significant changes in their health status.

TWO CASE STUDIES

Let's look at two examples and see what transpired in the lives of these people who were tested by the Social Readjustment Rating Scale:

Mary, a white female, age 25, worked in a local bank. In January she decided to marry (50 LCUs), leave her apartment and move to a new condominium (20), which had a mortgage over $40,000 (31). In June she became pregnant (40) and decided to quit work three months later (26). In November her father had a heart attack (44), and she went home each week to be with her mother (25). She drove to her own home each weekend to be with her husband and found little time for social activities (19). Mary's LCU score for that year was 255.

Such a score brought with it a 50% chance of increased illness. Mary experienced "more colds than average," one of which turned into a complicated sinus infection. She also reported insomnia many nights and claimed 10 sick days (twice the average rate) before she quit her job. Clearly the stress was getting to her. She had an overload.

Fred, a 50-year-old white male, was self-employed as an insurance broker. Fred's youngest daughter, Jane, was married in June and left home (29). In the process he gained a son-in-law (30). There was an unusual increase in the number of family get-to-gethers (his new son-in-law came from a large family) as a result of Jane's wedding and events surrounding it (15). As the top seller of a group-health insurance in his region, he was the winner of the coveted President's Award (28). Fred's LCU score for the year was 111. Despite the big wedding in the family, his score was well within normal. He noted no adverse effects on his health.

In my classes my associates and I have modified the original Holmes-Rahe instrument a bit. Two of the changes were due to the impact of inflation on Americans: life events 20 and 37 were upgraded from $10,000 to $40,000 to indicate a more realistic amount of mortgage money for homes.

Then, we made some changes in the last three items on the original Holmes-Rahe list: 41, "Vacation," 42, "Christmas," and 43, "Minor violations of the law." For these items our experiences indicated some other options were needed. Our version now reads: 41, "Single person living alone," and 42 and 43, "Other—describe." In each case an individual can give an appropriate number of points that reflect the amount of distress caused by a situation that may be personally traumatic —but not accurately covered by the events listed. Examples could include: "My roommate is on drugs, and we're having a lot of problems," 25 LCUs; or "My new job takes me away from home a lot," 10 LCUs. Although such events may be covered in an earlier category, the individuals we've worked with do not recognize the events in those terms. We also found that most people had problems with the terminology of the events as originally described by Holmes and Rahe.

TEST YOUR OWN STRESS

Now it's time for you to take our version of the Holmes-Rahe test, the Self-Test for Stress Levels. Remember to circle all the items which apply to you for events that have occurred in the last *12 months*.

SELF-TEST FOR STRESS LEVELS

Instructions: Circle each item which applies to you. Mark events that have occurred within the last 12 months. Enter total at bottom.

Life Event	Value
1. Death of spouse	100
2. Divorce	73
3. Marital separation	65
4. Jail term	63
5. Death of close family member	63
6. Personal injury or illness	53
7. Marriage	50
8. Fired at work	47
9. Marital reconciliation	45
10. Retirement	45
11. Change in health of family member	44
12. Pregnancy	40
13. Sex difficulties	39
14. Gain of new family member	39
15. Business readjustment	39
16. Change in financial state	38
17. Death of close friend	37
18. Change to a different line of work	36
19. Change in the number of arguments with spouse	35
20. Mortgage over $40,000	31
21. Foreclosure of mortgage or loan	30
22. Change in responsibilities at work	29
23. Son or daughter leaving home	29
24. Trouble with in-laws	29
25. Outstanding personal achievement	28
26. Spouse begins or stops work	26
27. Begin or end school	26
28. Change in living conditions	25
29. Revision of personal habits	24
30. Trouble with the boss	23

31. Change in work hours or conditions 20
32. Change in residence 20
33. Change in schools 20
34. Change in recreation 19
35. Change in church activities 19
36. Change in social activities 18
37. Mortgage or loan of less than $40,000 17
38. Change in the number of family get-togethers 15
39. Change in sleeping habits 15
40. Change in eating habits 15
41. Single person living alone .... °
42. Other—describe .... °
43. Other—describe .... °

° Give appropriate points yourself   Total _____
Source: Research done by Drs. T. H. Holmes and R. H. Rahe

How did you rate? What can you learn from it? Is the information valuable to you?

One of my friends and neighbors, Doug Nelson, (not his real name) found it to be most useful to him. Doug was an editor with a major publisher. His firm was bought by a New York firm, and he was offered a job—if he would move. So he rented his house and moved—after first getting married. After a year in Manhattan he'd had enough and moved back to his home. He no sooner moved back than he got another job offer with a big increase in pay—but it required another move. When he asked me what to do, I said, "Take the Self-Test for Stress Levels." By the time he had marked marriage, business readjustment, change in financial state, change in living conditions, etc., Doug had scored nearly 400 points. As he pondered the size of his score, the new job offer, and the stress another move would bring him and his wife, his decision took only a few minutes: "I'll refuse the job offer."

The value of this Self-Test for Stress Levels is that if you are getting totals of 300 and more, you are well-advised to take it easy for a year or so with any major decisions. Not making a decision to change is an acceptable option.

So now you have learned one way to answer the question, "How much stress is OK?" Your score may be high enough to suggest you've already had too much. Years ago, before the advent of today's mining safety devices, coal miners took canaries down into the mines with them. If there was a dangerous build-up of poisonous gases, these canaries would fall off their perches and alert the miners of the danger. The men could then get out in a hurry.

A score of over 300 in the Self-Test may indicate there is danger in your "coal mine." In Part II of this book, you will find many practical ways to get out in a hurry—to handle stress more effectively. But before that, there are some other ways to tell you if there is danger. One way is to learn to listen to your body talk to you. These ways are outlined in the next chapter.

7

Listen! Your Body Is Talking to You

When the red light is flashing on your automobile's dashboard, it tells you that your parking brake is on, and when the dial on the gasoline gauge signals empty, your car is "talking" to you. Such messages are protecting you from further action that could ruin your brake linings or leave you stalled in the middle of a busy highway. When such talk occurs, you listen and take action. Unfortunately, when their own bodies talk with flashing lights (symptoms such as headache, insomnia, or irritability), far too many people ignore them. If your energy sends the signal "empty" after stress overload—and you ignore it—you could end up "stalled"—not on the highway but in a hospital bed.

THE CASE HISTORY OF RITA

Let's look at the story of a young lady we'll call Rita Nelson. Her case history tells an all-too-familiar story about such body talk:

I first met Rita when I was helping prepare a television series for a national corporation. Company managers asked me to develop a medical self-care program emphasizing disease prevention and health promotion. I felt a good place to start might be to interview an employee who had recently been discharged from a hospital after recovering from a major illness. Sometimes that humbling experience of lying flat on one's back in bed in a hospital helps put the world in focus. I felt that talking to such an employee about the things that they might change in their lifestyle—given a second chance—would be an interesting way to start the TV series.

I called the personnel department and asked if anyone was in the hospital and would be willing to talk to me about their illness in front of a camera crew. A tough request!

Three days later the phone in my office rang. Arrangements had been made. The employee would soon be discharged from the hospital. Yes, the employee was willing to be on television. Yes, the doctor would give me the medical records. Yes, we could go to the employee's home for the filming.

I could just see the medical record in my mind's eye: "Patient brought to E.R. by ambulance. Diagnosis: coronary occlusion. One week in coronary care unit. One week in general medical ward. Patient's description: male, 52 years old, overweight, heavy smoker." So you can understand my surprise when the records arrived on the day I was to meet the employee:

"Female, 32 years old, mild hypertension, normal weight, hadn't smoked for one month."

That surprise was not the only surprise I got that day! The television crew and I arrived at her suburban home on a bright, sunny summer day. I rang the doorbell and a female voice said, "Come in. I'm out on the porch."

The cameraman, the soundman, the producer, and I all traipsed out to the porch for the interview, but there was a problem: Rita talked with great difficulty.

"What medication are you taking?" I asked.

She showed me a bottle containing 10 mg. Valium tablets. She talked in a slow, slurred, precise manner. "My doctor wants me to take one or two of these blue tablets four times a day. They make me feel good, but I talk funny." Rita was stoned!

The interview had to be cancelled. Rita was in no shape for her TV debut. "We'll be back in two days," I said as we packed up to leave, "but no Valium, please."

The crew and I returned in two days. Rita's body was now free of tranquilizers. Our interview resumed:

DOCTOR: Did you feel sick before your hospitalization?

RITA: Not really, but was tired all the time.

DOCTOR: What do you mean by tired?

RITA: Well, I'd sleep 10 hours and get up tired and I couldn't do any work that amounted to much.

DOCTOR: What did you attribute that to?

RITA: Well, I had a bad year and figured it was just my nerves. I went to the doctor and he gave me those same blue nerve pills.

DOCTOR: What do you call a "bad year"?

After some more probing I found out these things about Rita's bad year:

- Insomnia for six months (used 4 oz. of bourbon at bedtime as nightcap, which gave her slight hangover every morning).
- Divorced from husband of seven years.
- Took tranquilizers to work with her most of the time.
- Worked two jobs (at company plus moonlighted as cocktail waitress).
- Many headaches (partly controlled with aspirin).
- Poor appetite for a year (ate on the run).
- Missed appointments and seemed forgetful.
- New job at company (didn't like new boss).
- Too busy for any exercise.
- Father died two weeks before her heart attack.

When I had her complete the Self-Test for Stress Levels, she scored 394. Scores that high (over 350 points) predict with over 90% likelihood that illness or accident will occur in the succeeding months.

Could Rita have prevented her heart attack by listening to her body talk? My contention is *yes*, she could have. Had she been trained to do it, what might she have heard?

THE SYMPTOMS OF STRESS OVERLOAD

Dr. Rosalind Forbes, director of Forbes Associates, stress consultants in New York, has developed a conceptual diagram that depicts some of the symptoms that people like Rita may feel from stress overload.

There are also psychological signals that can tell you your body is reaching the point of stress overload:

- Decision making becomes difficult (both major and minor kinds).
- Excessive daydreaming or fantasizing about "getting away from it all."
- Increased use of cigarettes and/or alcohol.

The Forbes Continuum of Underload/Overload

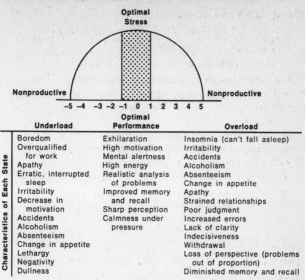

Characteristics of Each State	Underload	Optimal Performance	Overload
	Boredom	Exhilaration	Insomnia (can't fall asleep)
	Overqualified for work	High motivation	Irritability
	Apathy	Mental alertness	Accidents
	Erratic, interrupted sleep	High energy	Alcoholism
	Irritability	Realistic analysis of problems	Absenteeism
	Decrease in motivation	Improved memory and recall	Change in appetite
	Accidents	Sharp perception	Apathy
	Alcoholism	Calmness under pressure	Strained relationships
	Absenteeism		Poor judgment
	Change in appetite		Increased errors
	Lethargy		Lack of clarity
	Negativity		Indecisiveness
	Dullness		Withdrawal
			Loss of perspective (problems out of proportion)
			Diminished memory and recall

- Increased use of tranquilizers and "uppers."
- Thoughts trail off while speaking or writing.
- Excessive worrying about all things.
- Sudden outbursts of temper and hostility.
- Paranoid ideas and mistrust of friends and family.
- Forgetfulness for appointments, deadlines, dates.
- Frequent spells of brooding and feeling of inadequacy.
- Reversals in usual behavior.

One of the most common body signals is headache. Rita had them. As many as nine out of ten headaches arise from prolonged contraction of muscles in the head and neck: This comes about from the body's primitive "Fight or Flight Response." The body's muscles are ready to spring into physical action—but the action often never takes place because of social conditioning. Such contraction—which causes pain after a while—can begin after long hours of alertness, for example, while driving in heavy traffic or studying for a tough examination. They can also be caused by a home or job stress at work.

A do-it-yourself demonstration of muscle pain from prolonged muscle contractions will give you more insight into such pain or distress. Here's the demonstration:

1. Raise your arm high over your head.
2. Open and close your hand rapidly while counting to 20 slowly.
3. Now tightly clench your fist for another 20 seconds.
4. Lower your hand.
5. Look at the skin color of the palm of your hand.

You will feel stiffness, numbness, distress, and perhaps even pain from this simulation of musculoskeletal body talk. The pain came about by decreased blood flow and essential oxygen to the tissues involved. When you look at your hand, you will notice that it had a pale look for a few seconds before it pinked up when normal blood flow was restored.

The major cause of muscular and skeletal pain is the same for any part of the body: head, neck, upper back, lower back, shoulder. Once you have acquired a habit of tenseness for any group of muscles, when you overreact to stressful situations, there is lessened blood to the muscles and this can lead to chronic pain.

The Civil War diary of Gen. Ulysses S. Grant revealed how his headaches were triggered by a stressful situation and cured when the stressor was removed. When Gen. Robert E. Lee refused to cooperate on the eve before he was scheduled to surrender at Appomatox Courthouse, Grant experienced such a severe headache that he had to go to bed. When a messenger finally brought word that the Confederate leader had changed his mind, decided to cooperate, and even set the exact hour of the ceremony, Grant noted in his diary, "With wonderment, the pain in my head ceased."

What is the body trying to say to Rita—or to you—with pain, headaches, fatigue, insomnia, loss of appetite, or irritability? First of all, it is saying the same thing as the gauges and lights on your car's dashboard: "Something needs your attention. Some small action now will prevent big trouble later."

Unfortunately, many people don't know what their body is saying because of ignorance. Others may listen, but immediately turn off the useful and protective signals because they take pills such as aspirin or tranquilizers—often with the assistance of their doctors. Still others hear the signals but don't pay any attention to them because of their "Illusion of Immortality." ("Nothing could possibly happen to *me*.")

To help you learn to listen to your body's signals, I've included a test for you to take right now, the Self-Test for Stress Signals. This test on the next page will help you determine where you stand in regard to stress—and whether you might need to take urgent actions now!

SELF-TEST FOR STRESS SIGNALS

	Almost never	Infrequently	Sometimes	Frequently	Almost always
1. I can recognize anxiety, and keep it from interfering with my daily activities	1	2	3	4	5
2. I relax my mind and body without using drugs	1	2	3	4	5
3. I respect my own accomplishments..	1	2	3	4	5
4. I get enough satisfying sleep	1	2	3	4	5
5. I enjoy my life	1	2	3	4	5
6. I fall asleep in 20 minutes or less	1	2	3	4	5
7. I sleep soundly at night	1	2	3	4	5
8. I take enough time to eat	1	2	3	4	5
9. I am in control and not feeling "hyper" with mind and body going too fast	1	2	3	4	5
10. I can make decisions without difficulty	1	2	3	4	5

Total_____44_____

Analysis of Your Score

Total Score 40-50: You are treating your body very well. You are to be commended.

Total Score 30-40: Your life-style habits are good.

Total Score 20-30: There are some things that need adjustment. You had better ease up and listen more carefully to the signals from your body.

Total Score 10-20: You are not listening very well to your body. There are several danger signals turned on.

Part II

Managing Stress

8

Five Ways to Manage Stress

From Part I you have now learned what stress *is* and what it *isn't,* and the difference between *eustress* and *distress.* You have examined two major areas that can cause stress—the family and the job. You have learned to recognize the signs of stress, learned some of your body's danger signals, and to evaluate how much stress is probably OK. You've learned about the "causes" and the "casualties."

Now, you might ask, what about the "cures"? What can I do to control stress? Can I learn to manage my stress more effectively? Are there any remedies that I can use when things get out of control? Can an *ounce* of prevention cure a *pound* of stress?

Yes, with training and time, you can change stress to unstress. From my own experience as a family doctor and from my teaching of medical self-care methods to activated patients, I have identified Five Ways to Manage Stress.

Part II of this book will explore these Five Ways for you to learn to manage stress. Each will provide *expert knowledge* in *everyday language* that you can use.

But first, study the Pieces in the Puzzle of Stress Management. Each piece is so important that if one is missing, the solution to stress control is incomplete:

**The Pieces in the Puzzle
of Stress Management**

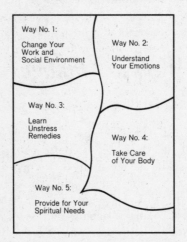

Way No. 1:
Change Your
Work and
Social Environment

Way No. 2:
Understand
Your Emotions

Way No. 3:
Learn
Unstress
Remedies

Way No. 4:
Take Care
of Your Body

Way No. 5:
Provide for Your
Spiritual Needs

Way No. 1: Change Your Work and Social Environment.

You will remember from Chapter 4 that people feel stress on the job especially when they have little control over duties and working conditions. Chapter 9, "Add More Control to Your Life," will show you how to analyze your work situation, reduce on-the-job stress, and gain greater satisfaction not only from your work but for your whole life.

In Chapter 3 you learned about the family under stress. In Chapter 10, "Renew Your Relationships," you will learn how to minimize distress in family relationships and to find greater happiness with both family and friends.

Way No. 2: Understand Your Emotions.

Most of us blame situations, people, and things "out there" for making us angry, sad, or distressed. Yet it is not the *outside* things that cause us stress but our *inside* perceptions that cause our "emotional cuts and bruises." Chapters 11 and 12 will help you understand the ABCs of your emotions and give you greater control over feelings like anger and anxiety.

Way No. 3: Learn Unstress Remedies.

Ways No. 1 and 2 can help control stress or, in some cases even prevent it. But what do we do when stress ties us in knots and makes us feel irritable and anxious? You will discover quick, simple, effective antidotes to stress in Chapter 13, "Relaxing with Massage," Chapter 14, "Ten Quick Relaxers," and Chapter 15, "Unstress Exercises."

Way No. 4: Take Care of Your Body.

You can manage stress more effectively when you are well fed, well rested, and well exercised. Chapter 16, "Nutrition and the Seven Golden Rules for Good Health," will summarize important health-promotion practices and medical self-care. Chapter 17, "Exercise: Your Safest Tranquilizer," will help you plan an exercise program that is right for you.

Way No. 5: Provide for Your Spiritual Needs.

Any successful approach to stress management must be holistic. It must be based on a view that sees you as having body, mind, and spirit. Chapter 18, "Spiritual Growth Through Prayer," explores the role of religion and how worship, prayer, and meditation are integral parts of any program of stress management.

Chapter 19 is the key to developing your individual plans and program. It will help you put together the Pieces in the Puzzle of Stress Management by showing you how to analyze your present life-style, clarify your life goals, and set your own priorities for stress management. The results will be your Personal Action Plan.

Finally, Chapter 20, "Unstress Places and Resources," will be your guide to further information about professionals who are in the "unstress business" and worthwhile books you might want to read.

9

Add More Control to Your Life

In Chapter 11, "The ABCs of Your Emotions," you will learn about the basic human need to be happily alive with a *maximum* of joy, pleasure, satisfaction, and self-fulfillment, and a *minimum* of needless pain, dissatisfaction, discomfort, and self-defeat.

In order to achieve this—and add more control in your life—you must consciously *add* some things in your life and *subtract* others. This concept is important to you because a major cause of job stress is lack of control.

Governor Charles Thone of Nebraska, a long-time friend of mine, told me recently, "The biggest difference between my job now as governor of Nebraska and that of Congressman for eight years is that even though I have much more responsibility now, I have more control of my life than I did in Washington."

This whole business of control reminded me of a delightful essay about vacations by Sam Newlund (*Minneapolis Tribune*, August 13, 1980): "I spend my time exactly as I see fit, reading, writing, sunbathing, walking, eating, sleeping, shopping for cantaloupe and suntan lotion in nearby Onamia near Mille Lacs Lake. The beauty of it is I do these things exactly when I feel like it—not a moment before or moment after.

"So I'm reading at 2 p.m. and my eyes get heavy. At that moment I put the book down and flop onto the bed for a snooze, maybe a half hour's worth. If I'm hungry I eat, if not I don't. If I feel like reading 'til 3 a.m., I do so . . . .

"In short, I can regulate my activities like E. Power Biggs delicately adjusting the stops on a pipe organ. I'm in complete *control!*"

TIME USE AND JOB STRESS

One management expert I know, Tor Dahl, Associate Professor, School of Hospital Administration, University of Minnesota and president of Tor Dahl & Associates, has looked at stress management from the point of view of time use by managers and employees. He found loss of control to be a major cause of stress.

Dahl has developed a process whereby people analyze their jobs, then he determines if the employee is:

- stressed yet satisfied
- stressed but unsatisfied
- not stressed yet satisfied
- not stressed but unsatisfied

The time spent in types of work is then calculated as the total percent of time perceived as "satisfied" and "unsatisfied." The percentages are entered on a form like this:

	STRESSED	UNSTRESSED	
SATISFIED	A) EXCITEMENT Estimate % of time stressed and satisfied: % *Sample task:*	B) COMFORT Estimate % of time unstressed and satisfied: % *Sample task:*	Total % of time satisfied : % (A+B)
DISSATISFIED	C) DISCOMFORT Estimate % of time stressed and dissatisfied: % *Sample task:*	D) BOREDOM Estimate % of time unstressed and dissatisfied: % *Sample task:*	Total % of time dissatisfied: % (C+D)
	Total % of time stressed: (A+C) %	Total % of time unstressed: (B+D) %	100%

Here's how to fill out the form:

1. Estimate, in percent, how your total time at work is distributed between the four categories listed based on the definitions given below.

2. List four tasks that you do that fit within the four categories, one in each, based on the sample tasks listed below:

   a. **Excitement**
   Tasks which you find most rewarding (really gets the adrenalin flowing!).
   Sample task: Making a successful presentation.

   b. **Comfort**
   Low-key tasks which you find enjoyable.
   Sample task: Reading my favorite professional journal.

   c. **Discomfort**
   Difficult tasks that you would like to avoid.
   Sample task: Firing an employee.

   d. **Boredom**
   Repetitious tasks that lack appeal.
   Sample task: Making Xerox copies.

3. Keeping in mind that A + B + C + D will always equal 100 percent, add all rows and columns and enter totals in the spaces provided.

In a recent study at a major national corporation, Dahl found these results when he studied representative employees:

The employees in Category A perceived their work as providing excitement. They also reported their jobs offered:

- change and growth

- achievement and recognition

- outward orientation

	STRESSED	UNSTRESSED
SATISFIED	(% of time) A) EXCITEMENT 19.2	(% of time) B) COMFORT 60.2
DISSATISFIED	(% of time) C) DISCOMFORT 8.4	(% of time) D) BOREDOM 12.2

Those individuals in Category B reported comfort and job satisfaction, noting that their jobs provided:

- intimacy
- sensory stimulation
- acceptance

The perceptions the people reported in A and B made them feel good about themselves and their work. They were "happily alive" with the positive feelings of "joy, pleasure, satisfaction, and self-fulfillment."

The results perceived for Categories C and D were on the other end of the scale: discomfort and boredom.

In Category C people noted this about their jobs:

- rejection
- alienation
- failure

In Category D they reported feelings of:

- sensory deprivation
- stagnation

Representative sets of words from the analysis helped describe the feelings of the employees:

	STRESSED	UNSTRESSED
SATISFIED	A) EXCITEMENT "Challenge I can handle."	B) COMFORT "A good balance."
DISSATISFIED	C) DISCOMFORT "I can't handle it."	D) BOREDOM "They ask too little of me."

COPING WITH JOB DISTRESS

When people find themselves in a job setting or personal situation in which they experience boredom (D), discomfort (C), or even downright pain, what do they usually do? How do they cope with the problem?

There are several actions they can use:

Action 1. Alter one's interpretation of the situation so that it has less importance and is less distressful. The most common way of coping is through altering their attitude by making philosophical statements such as "We're all in the same boat"; "Well, that's life"; or even, "It's God's will." People can also alter the significance of the problem by focusing on *inner* aspects of being with peaceful thoughts, rather than focusing on *outer* experiences and external pressures. This can be accomplished with the help of prayer and unstress exercises. Persons who develop such skills have increased mastery over their feelings and greater emotional tranquility.

Action 2. Change the circumstances causing the distress. This method Dahl calls "The American Way." Common statements that describe such actions include: "Get your act together," "Get organized," "Establish action plan," "Change the way we do it," or, "If it doesn't work, fix it!"

Action 3. Increase the tolerance for distress. This can be done through methods like these:

Fitness and training. Military officers and leaders have used this method for many years. The "boot-camp tradition" for marines and sailors has shown that men and women who are physically fit can better tolerate the strains of war. Furthermore, programs at West Point, Annapolis, and Colorado Springs show that physically fit cadets not only do better under stressful conditions, but even achieve better grades in the classroom. Military experience has shown the value of simulated combat situations and war games in helping military personnel overcome fear through demanding training maneuvers.

Support groups. Self-help groups, such as Alcoholics Anonymous, practice methods that would be described by Hans Selye as "altruistic egotism." Members of such organizations help others as they help themselves. Recovering alcoholics increase their tolerance for the disruptions of their emotional life—and the danger of "falling off the wagon"—through the support they give others. They often speak of such activities as "paying my dues." This same philosophy accounts for much of the success of Overeaters Anonymous, Parents Without Partners, Gamblers Anonymous, Widow-to-Widow, and other mutual aid societies—including those bound together to cope with distressful conditions such as cystic fibrosis, hemophilia, muscular dystrophy, physical disability, blindness, deafness, and other impairments.

Prayer, faith, sense of purpose. Throughout the history of mankind, people have been helped to survive turmoil and trouble with the help of prayer, faith, and a strong sense of purpose. Viktor Frankl in *Man's Search for Meaning* tells how he survived the horrors of Auschwitz with the help of prayer and his strong religious beliefs. He kept up his appearance—and spirits—by shaving every day, even though he often had to use scraps of old razors and pieces of glass. He kept up hope by imagining how he would spend his time with his wife, family, and friends when he got out. As he existed on a day-to-day diet of stale bread and a few bowls of gruel, he even imagined what restaurant they'd go to and what he'd choose from the menu. He prayed to God for the strength to survive—and Frankl did.

Other victims in concentration camps and prisoners of war camps kept their sanity—and hopes alive—by reciting hymns, remembering Bible passages, and saying prayers. Still others down through the ages were like the saints and martyrs who endured their distress in the belief that such virtue would be rewarded in heaven.

Emotional releases. One time-honored way to increase tolerance for emotionally rocky times is to participate in competitive sports, pound the table with one's fist, hit a punching bag, throw things against the wall, yell at your dog or kids. Anger at a boss or spouse can be vented on a nearby dish, with strokes at a golf ball, or kicks at an empty box. The releases of hitting, of shouting, or crying help relieve the intensity of feelings being held inside. And, finally, "talking it out" with a friend, family member, or fellow worker will help give a new perspective or uncover a workable solution to the problem. Negative feelings, if not changed to positive ones, can at least be altered to neutral ones.

Action 4. Avoid the problem. A time-honored method is simply to avoid the problem. People can "vote with their feet" and walk away. Individuals quit their jobs, spouses desert their families, and teen-agers run away. Employees report in "sick" or take "sick leave." Other people go on vacation or escape to the mountains, lakes, or seashore. Still others avoid their problems by daydreaming, or use the fantasy of books, movies, and television. Unfortunately, all too many others abuse alcohol, drugs, and tranquilizers to escape their actual or perceived troubles.

Action 5. Do nothing. One final option, practiced by many, many people is to *do nothing*. In such situations, the stress control is left to others!

FINDING GREATER SATISFACTION IN LIFE

When Tor Dahl & Associates did further studies of the differences between satisfied and dissatisfied people, they found representative behaviors in each group. Sources of satisfaction could be classified in a spectrum that ranged from *internal* private and personal matters to *external* altruistic actions in church and community. The behaviors involved family, work, leisure, and religion.

The sources of satisfaction identified included these:

Intimacy
- Seek and share the innocence of a child.
- Be alone and silent for half an hour every day.
- Walk along a beach with someone you love.
- Sit up all night with a friend who has a problem, even though you have an early appointment the next morning.
- Smile at someone.
- Pray for someone.
- Make love to someone.

Sensory Stimulation
- Spend a week in the wilderness alone or with your family. Cook your own freshly caught trout, sleep under the stars, and listen to the wind rustling through the trees.
- Go for a walk in rain and wind.
- Savor the aroma of a roast in the oven, the taste of a

fruit picked right off the tree, the sight of a full moon over a quiet lake, the feel of a furry pet, the sound of the ice cream truck on a hot day.
- Remember the sound of the church bells at Christmas time in your hometown, the first snow of winter, the first leaves in the spring.
- Read a book or newspaper in your favorite chair.

Acceptance
- Listen to all sides in a story and make a fair decision that everyone accepts.
- Ask someone for advice, listen to what is said, and follow it if you agree.
- Study a foreign language, keep at it, and eventually visit the country where it is spoken.
- Buy something wildly extravagant for yourself and for your spouse or friend.
- Go to a nice restaurant when you are too busy or too poor to do so.

Achievement/Recognition
- Do a job well.
- Resolve a complaint to everyone's satisfaction.
- Teach someone a task and see it being done right.
- Complete the planning of next year's activities for a group that you manage.
- Concentrate so hard on what you are doing that you lose all track of time.
- Fix your car.
- Complete one task that has been burdening you for a long time. Do this every day, until you are completely current and in control.
- Run your first mile.
- Take off excess weight and keep it off.
- Get rid of a bad habit and stay rid of it.
- Take up a good habit and keep it through iron discipline.

Change/Grow
- Take a course that improves your own skills.
- See how a task can be improved and implement the change.
- Change a policy or problem that interferes with productive functioning.

- Bring a new idea to the attention of your supervisor and see it being implemented.
- Take a child with problems on a trip to a desired place and stay for awhile, just the two of you.
- Collect anything: prints or paintings of a favorite artist, ship models, handcrafted pewter, etc. Become an expert on what you collect.

Outward Orientation

- Help someone with a problem.
- In the company of others, praise a fellow worker for a job well done.
- Praise somebody's moral strength, understanding, personality, mind, aesthetic ability, physical strength, hobbies, work, or appearance.
- Write a thank-you letter to a person who changed your life.
- Call an old friend you have not talked to for a long time.
- Do a great kindness for someone without that person knowing about it.
- Give some of your time to your church or synagogue or to a charitable fraternal or educational organization, and do not expect thanks in return.
- Attend your son's or daughter's or niece's or nephew's school concert, athletic meet, graduation ceremony, or other milestone event. Make a toast or speech at the celebration party.
- Give flowers to someone whom you admire and respect.

GAINING CONTROL

Individuals who find themselves in Category C or D can take control and move themselves to A or B by using activities and opportunities for service to others like those above. Rather than feeling trapped or hopeless and being unhappy or dissatisfied, they can actively gain control.

Other simple rules developed by Dahl help correct situations that produce stress on the job:

1. Do one thing at a time. Focus *only* on what you do. Do not look back, or ahead while you are working. Live in the *now*.

2. Do the best you can, and do not worry about the outcome. You have done your best.

3. Don't worry about things over which you have no control. Such worry is useless and self-destructive.

4. Don't feel closed in. Realize that there are always options for anything that you have to do.

5. Recognize your own limitations and within those boundaries set realistic goals for yourself.

6. When a crisis occurs, face it. Take constructive action and organize a proper response. Be flexible.

7. Be active and productive.

The control of one's life is often difficult. To many people, there are just too great a number of variables over which they have no control. These attitudes affect all of us, rich and famous, poor and not famous.

One night as I was watching Johnny Carson interview his guest, singer Bette Midler, on the *Tonight Show*, I heard him say that Midler, in person, seemed very shy at times.

Carson said that many describe him as a shy person when they meet him at a private party, and Johnny and Bette talked about the two personalities many entertainers have—one "on stage" and one "off stage." The difference, they agreed, was *control*. In off-stage situations, they feel out of control and perhaps shy. On stage, everything is focused on them—the lights, the music, the timing. They are in control, and they are confident.

I know how that feels. Perception makes a difference. The first time I was on the *Tonight Show*, I had a real feeling of panic as I stood behind the curtain and listened to Ed McMahon introduce me as the next guest of Johnny Carson. I thought to myself,

"What in the world *am I* doing here with about 15 million people watching!"

Then in a split second the solution came. I said, "You have two options: you can either blow it by looking at Carson as a big celebrity, or you can pretend you're talking to a man from Nebraska—who grew up with a lot of the same people you know—and went to school in Lincoln at the University of Nebraska."

I took the latter path, and we got along fine. Now years later, people who saw me that night say, "You didn't look a bit scared!" And I wasn't. I was in *control*.

10

Renew Your Relationships

One way we can move from stress to unstress is to gain greater control over our lives—both on the job and off. Another way is to learn some simple methods to take the stress out of our relationships.

The ideas in this chapter can be applied to family living, work situations, or to relationships with friends or neighbors. These methods can help you renew your relationships.

One of the best sources of such methods is *The Friendship Factor* by Alan Loy McGinnis, a family counselor and pastor in Glendale, California.

McGinnis tells individuals how to maintain and nourish friendships with the people they care for. He helps us understand the qualities of friendship we all should know—but often fail to apply in our dealings with our families, neighbors, and fellow Christians.

In one of his chapters, Dr. McGinnis uses a business term and describes friendship as a "valuable commodity." He reported on a study at Carnegie Institute of Technology which showed that only about 15% of a person's business and engineering success is due to technical knowledge and that 85% is due to "human engineering" skills, such as the ability to lead and influence people. In a related way, when people are discharged from their jobs in industry, only 20 to 40% are let go because they lack technical skills. Most of the 60% to 80% were fired because they lacked human relations skills.

With that in mind, friendships must be assigned a high priority, including "friendships" within the home. They will not just happen, but we can help them happen by using the Five Friendship Rules.

THE FRIENDSHIP RULES

Friendship Rule 1. Assign top priority to your relationships. Jesus placed great value on relationships. He chose to spend much of his time deepening his relationships with a few significant persons rather than preaching to crowds. His teachings—and parables—are filled with ways to befriend people and improve relationships. In a similar way, McGinnis points out that people should spend more of their time deepening their relationships with a few significant persons.

Friendship Rule 2. Cultivate transparency. Betty Ford, noted for her candor, indicated that if you are willing to be open, there will be people who cannot keep from loving you. Openness and honesty can literally be a "health insurance policy preventing both mental illness and certain kinds of physical sickness." Be willing to talk to your friends and family about your problems and seek their help. The Bible backs this up, "Confess your sins to one another, and pray for one another, that you may be healed" (James 5:16).

Friendship Rule 3. Dare to talk about your affection. When Thomas Jefferson wrote to his lifelong friend John Adams in 1819, he said, "Take care of your health and be assured that you are most dear to me." Ben Franklin said this about affection: "Speak ill of no man, but speak all the good you know of everybody." Your spouse, your children, and your friends need to hear you say "I love you."

Friendship Rule 4. Learn the gestures of love. Gestures and attentive acts show your loved ones that you care: the little bouquet of flowers a husband takes his wife at the bus depot or the regular evening walk the father takes with his daughter. Other examples are the good night kiss, the celebration of birthdays and anniversaries, the handshakes, hugs, and jokes at reunions. All these gestures gather "interest" in the "bank of love" and produce a ripple of good will with those we care for.

Friendship Rule 5. Create space in your relationships. People who have successful friendships allow their loved ones room to expand and grow. Many relationships have been stifled—or even ruined—because of overpossessiveness on the part of a friend. Someone once said, "No one worth possessing can be possessed."

HAVE YOU HUGGED YOUR KID TODAY?

During the entire 19th century and up until the 1920s, the death rate for infants in foundling homes and orphanages throughout the United States was nearly 100%! The medical term for this tragedy was the Greek word, *marasmus,* which means "wasting away."

In 1915 a New York pediatrician, Henry Dwight

Chapin, studied children's homes in 10 American cities and made this startling report: "In all but one institution, every infant under two years of age died." Another child specialist, Dr. J. H. M. Knox, from Baltimore, described a study of 200 infants admitted to various institutions. Almost 90% died within a year, and the 10% who survived, he observed, were taken out of the institutions and placed in the care of foster parents or relatives!

It was not until just before World War I that Dr. Fritz Talbot of Boston made an observation that finally determined the cause of those untimely deaths.

When Talbot visited the Children's Clinic in Düsseldorf, Germany, he admired the sparkling white, scrubbed, neat wards—neat, that is, except for an older lady carrying an infant on her hip as she worked about the place.

"Who's that?" Talbot asked the clinic director, Doctor Schlossman.

"Oh," the director observed, "that's Old Anna. When we have done everything we can for a baby and it is still not doing well, we turn it over to Anna, and she is always successful!"

Had Old Anna lived in America in the 1980s, she would have on her car the bumper sticker made popular by the Mental Health Association, "Have you hugged your kid today?" She knew what mothers have always known: infants need much caressing and holding. In additon to nutritious milk and healthy food, babies need large doses of a miracle drug—TLC (Tender Loving Care).

What had that American doctor learned from the old German nurse that is applicable today about stress management? Children, both the little kind and the bigger adult-sized ones, require the stimulation of affection to survive. Recent work by stress expert Dr.

Selye has given us the reason: our human senses, touch, sight, and sound, send messages to the brain and its master gland, the pituitary. When such messages are not received, organs and glands fail.

These organs, in turn, send distress signals to the pituitary gland which responds by secreting ACTH, which in circumstances such as this, through its anti-inflammatory action, limit the flow of blood. Adrenalin is depleted. The babies in the foundling homes became less resistant to bacteria and diseases in general, and they died. They died because, in the attempt to fight infections, hospital personnel put the little babies in clean gowns, wrapped them in clean sheets, put them in clean beds in clean rooms, and in the process isolated the children from an essential ingredient for survival—human touching and hugging.

From the experiences with the little foundlings we know that the absence of love can have disastrous effects. It is also true that adults without human connections have more illness and higher mortality rates.

People learn to love by being loved, by being hugged, by seeing altruistic actions. They achieve health by the ability to love, to work, to play, and to be connected to other humans in their immediate and extended families.

In *The Human Connection* Ashley Montague and Floyd Matson say this about love: "It is the ability by demonstrative acts, to confer survival benefits on others in a creatively enlarging manner. This means that by one's acts one not only enables the other to live but to live more fully realized than he would otherwise have been."

BUILDING FAMILY HARMONY

You can nurture family love and harmony by following some simple practices like these:

1. Be cautious with criticism. One of the first things I learned when I was a boy living in North Dakota was the saying of the Dakota Sioux: "Do not judge your brother until you have walked two weeks in his moccasins." All persons must strive for as much understanding of others as they grant themselves. Try to see things as your spouse or your children see them.

2. Allow for solitude. My daughter Sarah gave me a book, *The Magic of Walking*. In it are essays by authors such as Christopher Morley, Charles Dickens, Thomas Mann, and others, who describe the benefits of walking and hiking—to gain solitude. They describe the curative values of the solitude of the woods, the mountains, and the seashore.

3. Be a good listener. An old proverb tells a lot about being a good listener.

Shared joy is double joy;
Shared sorrow is half sorrow.

Good listeners encourage friends and families to talk about themselves. An example of this is the story about Benjamin Disraeli, Prime Minister of Great Britain and longtime opponent in Parliament of William E. Gladstone. Disraeli was known as a good listener. One night he sat next to the wife of a British official at a party. At the end of that evening she recalled, "When I left the dining room after sitting next to Mr. Gladstone, I thought *he* was the cleverest man in England. But after sitting with Mr. Disraeli, I thought *I* was the cleverest woman in England."

4. Show your anger. Probably the worst advice I got from my mother was carried in two sayings common to her times: "Big boys don't cry," and "Young gentlemen don't get angry." I shouldn't blame her, because they were the psychologically accepted teachings of her day. Nevertheless, as a result I have always had an unnecessarily hard time expressing my anger.

Many men of my age who received such advice now go around with the internal scars of suppressed anger: stomach ulcers and high blood pressure.

I've made some progress along those lines (although my wife may disagree). A recent example sheds some light on this. My eight-year-old nephew was visiting in our home. He was getting a bit too rough in playing with his cousins.

I warned him to quiet down and explained the rules we had about running in our house. When he repeated his actions—and was rude in the process—I got very angry, shook him vigorously, and sat him down in a chair in the corner of our family room.

After a few minutes I went back and talked with him about our rules, why they were set up, and why I got angry when they were broken. But more importantly I explained, "I was angry about *your actions*, but I still love *you*." He understood my anger, and we have gotten along much better since that encounter. I showed my anger, but countered it with an explanation of my feelings.

The human relations experts say that the value in talking about such experiences is the separation of how you *feel* about the event and the *behavior* of the person who created the bad feelings. Many family arguments begin when this separation is overlooked. As an example, let's listen in on an argument:

HELEN: You never pay attention to me anymore.

FRED: Honestly, Helen, I don't know how to make you happy. No matter what I do you are always complaining about the things I do.

And the Big Fight was on. From then on it became not an occasion to talk about anger or separation of feelings, but who was "right" and who was "wrong"!

The argument might have been more productive if it had gone like this:

HELEN: You know, Fred, I'm really feeling lonely and neglected these days. You've been gone every night this week.

FRED: I know that and I'm sorry, but I've got that big law case and I feel depressed and anxious because I know I'm going to lose.

Helen was feeling lonely. Fred was feeling depressed. Instead of making *accusations* about each other, they could have reached out for help and understanding.

5. Be willing to apologize. In the movie *Love Story* a great injustice was dealt to all human relations, especially those between men and women. Ali McGraw and Ryan O'Neal concluded their famous scene with this explanation: "Love means never having to say you're sorry." That conclusion is simply not true, according to expert McGinnis. He had this to say about an apology: "A true apology is more than acknowledging of a mistake. It is recognition that something you have said, or done, has damaged a relationship—and you are concerned enough about that relationship to want it repaired and restored."

Way No. 1 for managing stress is "Change Your Work and Social Environment." This involves improving your social environment and renewing the relationships you have with members of your family and your friends. This is an extremely important undertaking and should start today. Whose advice does one seek? Where should one start? Alan Loy McGinnis had some good advice about that: "Christ is our source for the art of relating to people and making friends."

11

The ABCs of Your Emotions

"*My wife* drives me to drink."

"I get a headache at work because of *my foreman*."

"Whenever *my daughter* acts the way she did today, she ruins my day!"

Most people think that distressful emotions are caused by external factors: the wife, the foreman, the thoughtless daughter. People tend to blame *others* for their emotional upsets, as in these typical case histories:

John, a 50-year-old accountant with a drinking problem, was also moderately overweight and smoked three packs of cigarettes daily. John drank primarily on weekends. He couldn't afford to use alcohol during the week because of his demanding work as an auditor for a major national accounting firm.

When John was first seen at a clinic, it was because of recurring stomach pains. The notes of his personal physician read: "The patient had gotten along on Rolaids for years but has never been treated for peptic ulcer or digestive problems." During the medical interview John reported that his stomach pains were more common on weekends. When asked the reason for this, he said, "My wife drives me to drink."

Katherine was 28 years old and unmarried. She was a parts assembly technician at a machine and tool company. Kate, as she preferred to be called, worked the 3 to 11 shift and had been with the company for two years.

She was first seen a month earlier in the emergency room of the nearby community hospital with the complaint of dizziness and severe headache. After some preliminary tests and later a referral to a psychiatrist, she was given a working diagnosis of tension headache. During the history and exam, Kate said, "I get a headache at work because of my foreman."

Ann was a 42-year-old housewife when her trouble started. She and her husband ran a dairy farm. In addition to her work on the farm and her family duties with three children, she represented a home-and-kitchen products company and sold to her neighbors in the county.

Ann visited her family doctor with the complaints of insomnia, fatigue, and increased irritability. Her physician established a diagnosis of "anxiety state" and wrote a prescription for a mild tranquilizer. He also made arrangements for Ann to see the staff psychologist. As Ann put on her coat and started to leave the office, she said, "I'll be pleased to get to the bottom of this problem. Whenever my daughter acts the way she did today, she ruins my day!"

John, Kate, and Ann had two things in common: they assumed that *other* people caused their distress and that their emotions were so complex that only professionals could understand and correct the problems involved.

UNDERSTANDING OUR EMOTIONS

If their assumptions were inaccurate, what recent research into human behavior has shed new light on the types of problems outlined in their case histories? During the last 15 years Albert Ellis of the Institute for Rational Living in New York, J. B. Rotter of the University of Connecticut, B. F. Skinner at Harvard University, and Maxie C. Maultsby of the Rational Behavior Therapy Center at the University of Kentucky, have all made significant discoveries that have clarified human behavior. They also pioneered in developing new therapeutic and training methods. These scientists showed that individuals with emotional troubles can prevent or even eliminate much personal emotional conflict. Such individuals can gain more control over their lives and achieve many of their life's goals with less distress and personal turmoil.

In a foreword to Maultsby's book, *Help Yourself to Happiness,* Ellis said: "If Dr. Maultsby correctly outlines the goals of human rationality—as I think he does —they boil down to the achievement by a 'rational individual' of two basic values or purposes: (1) remaining alive, or surviving for a goodly number of years and (2) remaining happily alive—with a *maximum* of joy, pleasure, satisfaction and self-fulfillment and with a *minimum* of needless or gratuitous pain, dissatisfaction, discomfort and self-defeat."

I learned about Maultsby and his co-workers in Kentucky in 1978 and started reading about their methods. Later my wife, Colleen, and I went to Lexington to confer with them firsthand.

As Maultsby talked to me about "The ABCs of Your Emotions," he drew a beautiful and simple analogy: the horse and its rider. In this model, the "rider" (the thinking part of the brain, the "word brain") receives information from its sense organs (the eyes, the ears, nose, taste buds, skin), and the "horse" (the limbic part of the brain that controls gut feelings) goes wherever it is directed. Another way to say this is that one's Feeling Brain (the horse) is always directed by one's Thinking Brain (the rider).

YOUR EMOTIONAL ABCs

The Rider's Senses	A. Your perceptions are what you notice (see, hear, touch, taste).	SENSE ORGANS
The Rider	B. Your evaluative thoughts—self-talk, thinking (positive, negative, or neutral) about your perceptions.	NEO-CORTEX
The Horse	C. Your gut or emotional feelings—positive, negative, or neutral—that are triggered and maintained by your thoughts (anger, excitement, depression, anxiety).	LIMBIC SYSTEM

Let's pretend you are out hiking in the country. All of a sudden, a snake glides across your path. Your major sense organs, your eyes and ears, alert you to the snake. In a split second your Thinking Brain evaluates the situation and gives you three basic actions that are positive, neutral, or negative. These, in turn, direct your Feeling Brain.

If, for instance, you had been trained as a zoologist, you might be intrigued to see a water snake so far from a river or pond. You could then have a *positive* feeling, a curious or scientific one. If you had been frightened as a child and told all snakes were bad and dangerous, your action could be one of fear, a *negative* feeling. Based on past experiences as a hiker, you could also have a *neutral* feeling. You then would merely take two steps to the side, ignore the snake and continue on your way.

Another example of a common response can be seen in the office of the Acme Business Corporation where you can see Fred Fuming, one of the purchasing agents, angrily answering his phone. The voice on the other end of the phone has just told Fred that the truck from Detroit with the material that had been shipped RUSH was going to be late. Fuming has been purchasing agent for two years, and there had been many late shipments before. Why such an angry response this time? It was because the voice on the other end of the line came from the new assistant plant manager, Bob Smith. There had been bad feelings ever since Bob got the job that Fred Fuming had expected to get. Fred had been frustrated and depressed ever since he heard the news two weeks ago. The knowledge of the late shipment merely triggered the pent-up anger. It wasn't what Smith had actually said: it was Fuming's *perception* of what he heard that led to the anger.

Our perception of any event will determine our emotional response. The sensation of raindrops on your forehead can bring about a *negative* emotion—if you are a tennis player about to embark on a long-scheduled match with your friend. On the contrary, if you are a drought-stricken farmer, it can be a *positive* —even overwhelmingly joyful—emotion. If you are a secretary on the way to work, those raindrops can trigger a *neutral* emotion, a slight inconvenience.

DEVELOPING EMOTIONAL HABITS

Emotional habits — like all habits — have to be learned, and they can also be "unlearned." A good example of how habits are learned can be seen in the process a person goes through in learning to drive a car. Let's use the A-B-C model to understand what transpired when Dan Drew started his quest to get a driver's license.

Dan was 17 before he started to drive. He had lived with his parents in Turkey (his dad was with the U.S. Army) and had not had access to a family auto until Dan and his family returned to the States during his senior year in high school. His father wanted him to develop good driving habits, so Dan was enrolled in the Ace Driving School. Now let's follow Dan on his first day.

A. Dan's senses "perceived" the training car. His *eyes* looked at its color, size, and so on. His *hands* touched the door handle as he opened the door and got in. As the instructor gave the rundown on starting the car, Dan's *ears* listened carefully.

B. Dan's evaluative, that is, correct car-driving thoughts (self-talk) began: "First, I'm to put gear stick in P (park). Second, I put my left foot on the brake and turn the ignition key to the right. I wait a few seconds for the motor to run, and I shift the stick to D (drive) while my left foot is still on the brake pedal. Then, I look out the window to check the traffic. When there's no traffic, I'll be ready to start. Then I'll push my right foot gently on the gas pedal."

C. The novice driver's gut feelings were now triggered. Dan noticed mild apprehension (a normal healthy reaction to this new and potentially dangerous learning experience) as he rubbed together the slightly moist palms of his hands. If he had not been so busy, he would have also noticed an increased pulse rate. His sympathetic nervous system was on the job, but still everything was pretty much under control. Dan took a deep breath as he pulled away from the curb. He was experiencing a *positive* emotional feeling.

"So far, so good," Dan said as he progressed with his driver education. With daily practice over the next few weeks, he quickly learned safe, correct driving skills. After a month of experience he didn't have to think consciously: "First, gear stick in park. Second, foot on brake. Third, turn ignition key." He had learned "driving habits." In the process he didn't go A-B-C, he could go A-C or B-C. Dan no longer had to follow the robot-like steps the instructor had shown him. His brain converted the learning experience into a mental process we describe as *habit*.

But what if this had happened instead of event C above:

C. Dan was pulling away from the curb, and just as he started to relax a bit, a huge truck came hurtling at him. A near collision occurred! Before the instructor could stop it, Dan's car hit the fender of a parked car in front of them. When this terrifying experience was over, Dan was really shaken up. He decided that was enough for his first day. Dan had a *negative* emotional experience. It would take some time to alter that, but with time and practice he "unlearned" his initial negative experience, which could have turned into a fear of driving. He became a good, safe driver. Dan regained his confidence because he had developed a right *belief* and *attitude*.

Dr. Maultsby has developed some clear definitions and explanations of habit, belief, and attitude that I have found useful in understanding human emotions and behavior:

Habit
- A habit is an A-C or B-C mental process. It can provide physical as well as emotional actions.
- Emotional habits—like physical habits—must be learned and can be unlearned.
- Habit learning requires time and diligent practice.

- Habit unlearning requires *more* time and *more* diligent practice.

Belief
- A belief is a *spoken form* of habit.
- Beliefs are A-B mental connections of repeated perceptions of A.
- Persons always notice their beliefs because they have to *think* them through before they *speak* them.

Attitude
- An attitude is an *unspoken belief.*
- Persons usually don't notice them because they *don't have to think* them through.
- Most persons explain attitudes as *spontaneous* reactions, such as, "He made me feel good."

We use these words in sentences like these:

1. *Habit:* Dan developed the driving habit of signaling with his blinker light whenever he pulled away from the curb and then looking twice for traffic, first in the rearview mirror and then out the driver's window.

2. *Belief:* Each Sunday Helge repeated his belief in the words of the Apostles' Creed, "I believe in God, the Father Almighty. . . ."

3. *Attitude:* As a little child, Mary developed the attitude from the comments she heard from her Uncle Bill that all black people were lazy.

CHANGING EMOTIONAL HABITS

With these definitions and concepts to help us understand the Emotional ABCs, let's go back and study the case histories of John, the problem drinker; Kate, the worker who was uptight about her boss; and Ann, the troubled housewife.

Did John's wife "drive him to drink" or was it his *perception* of what he heard and saw? The negative emotions he had built up through the years led to his abusing alcohol in an effort to drown his negative emotions about himself and his irrational fears of the world about him. John had not learned how to feel better *without drinking*. Alcohol clouded his emotions and let him feel irrationally hopeful about things he was afraid of when sober. With counseling, abstinence from alcohol, and long-term help from Alcoholics Anonymous, John recovered. He also learned many ways to feel good without drinking alcohol. He and his wife are getting along well. He was recently promoted and received a salary increase at the office. John is grateful that he kicked his alcohol habit.

Did Kate "get her headaches" from her boss? When she studied her emotional ABCs, she was able to identify the reason she was uptight with Stan, her foreman. She realized she had significant problems relating to her father and many other "father figures" such as Stan—particularly if they were the authoritarian type. With counseling and insight, Kate eventually learned to move many of her negative feelings over on the scale to a more neutral position. Even though she never brought herself to like Stan, at least she didn't get the severe tension headaches that developed from her negative feelings.

Ann, the troubled housewife, had difficulty in working out the relationship she had with her 17-year-old daughter, Jane. Over the last three years Ann's insomnia, irritability, and chronic fatigue had taken its toll. She had gained a lot of weight—40 pounds to be exact—because whenever she was irritable she went straight to the refrigerator. The more she gained, the less she felt like doing things. She became sedentary and out of shape, and puffed even when she walked upstairs. She even took up smoking Virginia Slims in a mistaken attitude that they would help her lose weight.

Her faulty relationship with her daughter turned out to be, in part, a common and normal conflict between teen and parent as Jane asserted her need for independence.

With help from the staff psychologist, several of the parent-teen conflicts were worked out. Unfortunately Ann had gained weight and lost self-esteem in the process. She was still so uncertain about her ability to change that the psychologist labeled the outlook for recovery as "guarded at best. Long-term therapy needed."

One of Ann's problems was that she distrusted her thoughts and her ability to control her emotions. Her problem is not hers alone. Many people distrust their thoughts—their evaluative thoughts—because thoughts are painless, easily changed, and ephemeral, while gut or emotional feelings can be so intense and seemingly uncontrollable.

Many persons with such experiences blindly trust their feelings—even though they are causing great distress. It is because of such distrust and inaccurate perceptions that many lay people have been reluctant to take charge and try medical self-care methods. However, with the self-tests and methods presented in the next chapter, you can start to be in charge—and feel better about yourself and the people around you.

12

Who's in Charge Here?

When I was in the U.S. Navy during World War II, the chief petty officer of our unit was making his rounds at 2400 hours. As he approached my watch post on the first night I served it as an apprentice seaman, he asked me in a brusque voice, "Who's in charge here?" When I said, "I don't know," the chief replied, "Well, you better find out before I return!" After he'd been gone about five minutes, I quickly found out by searching for the answer in the *Naval Regulation.* After 2300 hours, I was!

Just as *I was in charge* at an obscure post at midnight in 1944—even before I knew it officially—*you are in charge* of your emotional feelings—even if you don't realize it.

In addition to this, it is possible for people to improve their emotional control of feelings, to control themselves rationally. The problem is that the majority of people have not learned such control because knowledge about it has been available only in recent years.

After you understand the concept of the Emotional ABCs, the first step in control is to learn to use the Self-Test for Rational Living. These questions are based on the methods developed by Maultsby and his co-workers at the University of Kentucky. The questions are used in evaluating feelings surrounding an event or situation that caused negative emotions or anxiety. They can also be used to set priorities or rate the importance of an event. The Self-Test is also helpful in the decision-making involved in solving problems related to the event.

THE FIVE RATIONAL QUESTIONS

These are the five questions to ask regarding a thought (self-talk) related to the event:

1. Is the thought true and based on objective facts and events?
2. Will the action taken protect you from probable harm?
3. Will it help you achieve short and long-term life goals?
4. Will it help avoid significant emotional conflict with others?
5. Will it help avoid significant emotional conflict and negative feelings with yourself?

If, after conducting an analysis of the event, you find the answer is "yes" in three of the five questions, then the event was important enough (that is, upsetting enough) to conduct a Self-Test to help you decide on a plan of action. (It must be emphasized here that *very few* of the emotional cuts and bruises we experience can be answered yes to three of the five questions. The vast majority of common events, though they may really hurt and often cause the upset we call an anxiety state, don't warrant the emotional distress we have *learned* to lay on ourselves. Though such long-established emotional habits are difficult to change, they can be *unlearned*.)

SELF-TEST FOR RATIONAL LIVING

A. FACTS AND EVENTS
   (Describe here in simple language the facts of the event that you are analyzing.)

B. SELF-TALK
   (Write down all the thoughts you had in or about the event you described in A.)
   B1.
   B2.
   B3.

C. FEELINGS
   (State your feelings about A; i.e., "I felt angry, depressed, etc.")

Da. CHALLENGE TO A
   (If you put anything in the A section that is not factual, correct it here.)

Db. CHALLENGE TO B
   (Challenge each thought in B according to the five characteristics of rational thinking.)
   D1.
   D2.
   D3.

E. WAY I WANT TO FEEL
   (Write a simple statement describing how you want to feel in the future about this kind of situation.)

Here's how Kate in Chapter 11 used the Self-Test:

A. FACTS AND EVENTS
   My foreman really chewed me out for something. I didn't do what he said I did. I didn't defend myself.

B. SELF-TALK
   B1. He's a jerk.

Da. CHALLENGE TO A
   My first sentence is utter nonsense. My boss didn't chew me out but merely told me what he thought was true. I was rational enough to try to protect my job, even though I was irrational enough to give myself a headache.

Db. CHALLENGES TO B
   D1. "He's a jerk" is an

119

untrue statement. It's not based on objective fact. He's not a jerk! He's a human being who behaved in a jerky way, in my opinion.

B2. I'm a gutless little girl for not sticking up for myself.

D2. "I'm a gutless little girl" is not true. It's not based on objective fact. I'm a 28-year-old woman.

B3. I always get blamed for everything.

D3. "I always get blamed for everything" is an exaggeration and is not true. I rarely get blamed. By thinking I *always* do, I make an unfortunate event appear to be a terrible thing.

B4. Nobody cares about me.

D4. "Nobody cares about me" is not true. I care about me and I'm somebody. My brothers and sisters and boyfriend care about me.

C. FEELINGS
Anger, depression

E. WAY I WANT TO FEEL
Calm
Desired actions:
Avoid headache; forget about boss.

After Ann in Chapter 11 had worked out some of her family problems with the help of the psychologist, she decided to do a Self-Test about her eating habits. It looked like this:

A. FACTS AND EVENTS
I am watching my favorite TV show. There is a commercial for sundaes.

Da. CHALLENGE TO A
This is a fact.

B. SELF-TALK
B1. A sundae would taste so good.

Db. CHALLENGES TO B
D1. *RQ 1°* No, it is true that I like the taste, but I'm implying that I have to have it because I like it, and that's *not true.*
RQ 2 No, this leads me

° See Rational Questions, page 118.

to want what is not good for my health.

RQ 3 No, this does not help me change my eating habits. My goal now is to say no to my craving.

RQ 4 DNA°

RQ 5 No, I want to feel good about saying *no* to my craving. This helps me feel good about something that is bad for me.

B2. It won't hurt to have a sundae. I can start my diet tomorrow.

D2. RQ 1 No, a sundae adds calories and sugar and that means poor nutrition and overeating.

RQ 2 No, it will hurt my body in the sense that the more I eat, the more physical risks I take.

RQ 3 No, my goal is to stop eating when I am craving. A sundae only feeds the crave.

RQ 4 DNA

RQ 5 No, I want to feel calm when I think of food.

B3. I deserve something good to eat because I've been "good" for several days.

D3. RQ 1 No, eating is only a reward to me because I have learned to make it a reward. Eating is not a logical consequence of being good.

RQ 2 No, this idea leads to overeating and that is not good for my health.

RQ 3 No, eating encourages eating. This kind of thinking will work against my goal of changing my eating habits. A reward is good, but not food.

RQ 4 DNA unless I expect people to reward me with food and get grouchy when they don't.

RQ 5 No, this idea makes

° Does Not Apply.

C. FEELINGS
   Urge to eat, tense, depressed

E. WAY I WANT TO FEEL
   Calm, relaxed, enjoy the TV show
   Desired actions:
   Focus on the TV show, forget the food.

me feel good about irrational eating, and I want to feel good without eating.

(Adapted from Dr. Maultsby's newsletter, *Interaction*, Vol. 7, No. 3, August, 1979.)

Ann did her Self-Test in a slightly different way than Kate did. She wrote the answers to the Rational Questions, RQ 1, RQ 2, etc. directly into the format she used. Here is what she learned about each of the questions she asked herself:

RQ 1. Is the thought true and based on objective facts and events?

When she pictured the event, she asked herself if a television camera crew had been there and could show her an immediate rerun (as they do with action in football games), what actually happened? There was no problem in establishing the facts, so she wrote her answers.

RQ 2. Will it protect you from probable harm?

Ann asked herself, Will the actions that follow do me actual harm (that is, will it hurt my body or endanger my health in some way)? She agreed that her habit of overeating made her overweight and might shorten her life expectancy.

RQ 3. Will it help you achieve short and long-term life goals?

She reasoned that the action taken would make it difficult for her to reach short-term goals (in Ann's case, the loss of 40 lbs.) and long-term goals such as a maximum of happiness and joy.

RQ 4. Will it help avoid significant emotional conflict with others?

Ann put down "DNA" (does not apply). That is probably a correct answer for her Self-Test. (However, if her action had been related, for example, to alcohol abuse, it could have led to a significant blow-up with her spouse or family or employer—with very significant emotional conflict.)

RQ 5. Will it avoid significant emotional conflict or negative feelings with yourself?

It is usually easy to tell whether an interpersonal event will create negative feelings for yourself. Ann answered her question by saying *no* and still feeling good about saying it.

Because of the insight and control that Ann gained from her Self-Test, she was able to go one step further. After she had provided the rational challenges already noted, she added another column to her format. After she had forgone her habitual raid on the refrigerator to fix her sundae, she added these remarks as Rational Alternative Self-Talk:

Rational Alternative Self-Talk

1. I do not need an ice cream sundae now. I want to change my eating habits. I am not a slave to the taste of a sundae. I want to do what I know is good for me. Therefore, I say *no* to the sundae now; and I feel good about doing what is good for me.

2. I will start changing my eating habits right now. I do not need to eat; I do not want to eat; I refuse to eat. I will calmly continue what I'm doing and forget about the sundae.

3. Human beings do not have to be "good" to deserve to eat. Eating is a human activity, and I do not have to earn it. However, it is not good for me to eat now. I choose to change my habits and stop my cravings. Therefore, I'm going to say *no* to a sundae now and focus on my TV show.

Ann, John, and Kate found ways to "be in charge." They learned Way No. 2 for managing stress: *Understand Your Emotions*. You can learn to be in charge of your emotions too.

13

Relaxing with Massage

For centuries people from all parts of the world have used various types of massage to heal and relax themselves and their families and friends. You can do the same. But where do you start?

One of the best ways I know is that worked out by Larry Clingenpeel, a friend in Torrance, California. Larry is a Certified Massage Technician and has prepared several massage techniques that focus on:

1. Hand
2. Foot
3. Neck
4. Face/scalp

His techniques may be applied singly or as a total relaxation sequence. Practice each alone, and then as you get more experienced, with a family member or friend. The techniques can be expanded and adapted as needed. The only materials needed will be an ounce of coconut oil (or baby oil) in a small bowl, and a small towel—plus your fingers and hands.

Have the subject sit in a comfortable position or lie on the floor with his or her face up. You may want to set the mood of relaxation by turning on the radio or phonograph, selecting some soft, mellow music.

Do the massage in a slow, deliberate manner. Encourage the subject to inhale and exhale slowly and deeply during the massage. Such deep breathing encourages relaxation. When you are a bit too vigorous, you will hear complaints such as: "Not so hard" or "Slower, please." When you're doing it just right, you will hear these compliments: "That feels so good," or you may only hear a relaxed "Ahhh."

HAND METHOD

1. Take one hand of the individual and with the palm up—in your hand—add a small amount of oil to your fingers.

2. Stroke the palmar surface of the subject's hand with both your thumbs for a few moments and then stroke the surface of each finger, starting with the little finger and ending with the thumb.

3. Now rotate each finger joint while gently pulling it.

4. Next pull each finger and let your fingers gently slide off the tips of the subject's. (If there is too much oil on the fingers to permit gentle pulling, dry hands with towel.)

5. Repeat entire sequence with other hand of individual.

FOOT METHOD

Before starting the massage, make sure the feet of the subject are clean and free of open cuts or sores and skin conditions such as athlete's foot (fungus dermatitis) or other evidence of infection. Ask the person if there are any painful or sensitive areas while you are massaging the soles of his or her feet.

1. Put a small amount of oil into your hands and rub it on the first foot.

2. Lift the ankle with one hand and rub the back of the heel with the other.

3. Use both thumbs in long, wide strokes. Stroke over the bottom of the foot and then pull off the ends of the toes. Use light pressure and determine the level that feels good to the subject.

4. Hold both sides of the small toe, rotate it twice clockwise and pull gently. Then repeat this to each of the other toes.

5. Gently pinch the side of the foot and the tip of each toe, starting with the small toe.

6. With both thumbs held next to each other, press into the foot starting at the base of the big and second toes. Continue this down the inside of the foot to the heel.

7. Use a thumb-over-thumb (one on top of the foot and one on the bottom) in a pinching stroke. Make pinches up the bottom of the foot and off the end of a toe. Start with the inside of the foot with the small toe and end with the big toe.

8. Start at the base of the big toe, stroke across the sole of the foot with your thumb and then back across the foot just below the first stroke path. Repeat this all the way down to the end of the heel.

9. Use the tips of the fingers to apply pressure and make several circular strokes around the ankle, then continue this circular motion over the top of the foot.

10. Start with the big toe and bend it toward the top of the foot with one thumb and then bend it down

over the sole several times. Repeat this with each toe. Be gentle, because most toes are stiff.

11. Hold the ball of the foot with the hand on that side and hold the ankle with the other hand. Make two slow circles each way with the ball of the foot to rotate the ankle joint.

12. With the person's leg held straight, do a "gastroc stretch" of the calf of the leg by putting one hand under the ankle and the palm of your other hand on the upper half of the sole of the foot. Raise the leg up and hold the stretch for 15 seconds. Be gentle. Ask the person if the stretch was long and hard enough; if not, adjust accordingly. Most people have tight gastrocs (the calf muscles).

13. Rub the foot briskly with the towel to remove the oil.

14. Repeat procedure on the other foot. Sensitive areas of feet should be worked lightly and for a longer time.

NECK METHOD

1. Have individual receiving massage lie on his or her back, face up on the floor with head on a small pillow.

2. The person giving the massage kneels at the head of individual. Knees are placed on each side of the head and gently touch the shoulders.

3. Reach under back of head and locate reflex points (the occipital protuberance) on each side at base of skull, as in the drawing on page 129. You can locate them by feeling the base of the skull behind the ear and then move toward the spine. Follow the lower edge of the skull until you come to a slight notch or depression between the tendons of two muscles about 1½″ from the midline. There is one of these points on each side.

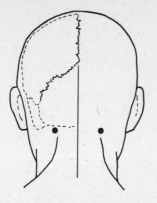

4. Apply firm pressure with your thumbs to each reflex point for 15-20 seconds. If it is quite tender, continue applying pressure until pain or tenderness decreases or disappears completely.

5. Now drop down along the sides of the neck for about 2½" in the same trough between the muscles and you will find the next pair of reflex points, one on each side of the neck at the level of the third cervical vertebra. Apply pressure with thumbs for 15-20 seconds. Then apply small amount of oil to neck area and massage gently.

6. Now move to the third location, at the level of the second thoracic vertebra in the upper part of your back. The location is 1½ inches lateral to the midline, about an inch inside of the border of the shoulder blade, as in the drawing below. Apply firm pressure to reflex points with thumbs for 15-20 seconds.

To reach this location, it may help to remove the pillow from under the individual's head and gently support the head with your hands.

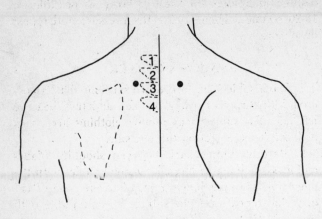

FACE AND SCALP

1. Have subject sit upright in a chair. The person giving the massage should stand behind the chair.

2. Apply a small amount of oil to the forehead and then gently stretch skin of forehead with index finger, moving in circular patterns.

3. Use index and third fingers to gently massage around the orbital bones of the eyes in a circular motion. Continue massage of entire facial area, stroking and gently stretching the skin.

4. Next, apply the ear pull by grasping ear between thumb and index finger. Gently tug down, then up, then sideways. Then do the other ear.

5. Now do the scalp massage and stretch scalp on head. Cover entire surface of head.

6. Finally, do the head squeeze. Have the individual sit straight upright in chair and then place the palms of your hands over both ears. Press inward against the skull as firmly as you can for 15-20 seconds. Then release the pressure and repeat once more. Next, put one hand on the forehead and the other

over the back of the head. Press inward with both hands and squeeze the skull as firmly as possible for 15-20 seconds. Then release the pressure and repeat once more.

NECK AND BACK

1. Have subject lie face down on floor that is covered with carpet or heavy blanket, and turn head to left side. The subject may remove clothing from back or leave it on. Kneel on the left side.

2. Start on upper back between shoulder blades and massage the area by making small circles with the fingertips. Massage slowly upward to the base of the neck and repeat until the subject is comfortable with pressure.

3. If subject has removed clothing and back is bare, put some oil on your hands and fingers and work it in well. It will aid in the massage process.

4. Slide both hands upward on the subject's left side along the entire spine to the hairline on neck. Gently lift the head and neck up from the floor. Lower head and turn it to the right.

5. Make a Y with right thumb and index finger, and then with kneading and gentle pinching actions move hand down entire left side of subject from below left shoulder blade down to small of back.

6. Now move to other side and kneel on right. Make Y with left thumb and index finger and repeat same kneading and gentle pinching actions along left back from shoulder blade to low back.

7. Provide general vigorous massage to entire right side of back with both hands. Make small circles with fingertips.

8. Repeat action to entire left side. Add oil to hands if needed.

9. Finish with gentle massage using fingertips to do light strokes from midline outward. Start at the hairline of the neck and end at the small of the back. In order to be comfortable, kneel on right for right side and on left for left side.

Which reminds me, I haven't had a back rub for quite a while, so pardon me while I enlist the help of my wife, Colleen, and see if the "First Aid Kit" in her hands is still working!

14

Ten Quick Relaxers

I once taught a health activation class for school children in Washington, D.C. One of my sessions dealt with teaching these grade schoolers about body talk and symptoms. We talked about the symptoms associated with stressful situations, and asked if any of them had had such experiences. Surprisingly, about half of them had!

One told how he got sick to his stomach when he had to hurry to get to school on time. One bright-eyed, dark-haired girl reported that she frequently got headaches when her dad drove her home from school in Washington's afternoon rush-hour traffic. Another student recalled how she got so angry at her mother in an argument about cleaning up her room that she vomited on the floor!

When we got to Tyrone, a handsome, black 11-year-old, he said, "If you're looking for Mr. Tension, he don't live at my house!"

As the class howled with laughter, I asked, "Why not?"

Tyrone responded, "Because my mom done run him out!"

If Mr. Tension shows up at your house, with the Quick Relaxers presented in the next few pages, you'll be able to *run him out!*

The first parts in the "unstress" process should already be fixed in your mind from what you've already read. Those steps are the preventive ones described in earlier chapters:

- Putting more control in your life
- Taking the stress out of your personal relationships
- Understanding your emotional ABCs
- Learning to heed the signals of stress

Such preventive actions should start becoming a part of your everyday life over the months and years ahead. There will, however, be "those days" when things get out of hand, when events in your life and those you care about swing out of control. The Quick Relaxers described in this chapter will help you get off the Hurry-Flurry Merry-Go-Round for a few minutes.

How do you spot Mr. Tension in the first place? What are your body's built-in warning signals when stress levels are getting dangerously high? Common early signals that you might experience include:

- A "keyed-up" or "wound-up" feeling
- Muscle tightness or pain in neck or shoulders
- Uptight feeling in pit of stomach
- Pain in forehead
- Rapid shallow breathing
- Dry throat and difficulty in swallowing
- Tenderness and dryness in nose

Each individual has his own warning signal or body talk. In my case, the first signal I can spot is tenderness and dryness in my nose. Later on I will usually experience an uptight feeling in the pit of my stomach. The first signal is caused by spasm of the tiny arteries in the mucous membrane of my nose. The second signal is caused by spasm of the smooth muscle in my stomach. Both my nose and stomach are target areas that have been stress spots all my life.

My wife, Colleen, reports that her first warning signal is a pain in the frontal sinus areas of her forehead. Later she will feel pain in the back of her neck.

Whatever your warning signal, learn what it is and then *pay attention to it*. It means that you may need to take time out from a stressful situation.

Here are some self-care methods you can learn to use:

QUICK RELAXER 1.   THE CATNAP

There are stories of military commanders, such as Napoleon, who actually took catnaps during their battles and awoke refreshed. You too may have to take time out from a stressful situation at home or work—if not an actual battlefield—in order to recharge your batteries.

For the record, I have always been a "catnapper"— dating back in my medical school days when I would "catch five" during lights out while the chairman of the anatomy department showed us slides or the professor of biochemistry dazzled us with charts depicting the intricacies of pyruvic acid.

After surviving my stress-filled medical school years first at the University of South Dakota and later at Case Western Reserve University, I became a "certified catnapper." I've taken naps everywhere: on the examining table in my family practice offices, on airplanes, in cars, on the floor of my office at Georgetown University. I've napped on hiking trails, logs, rocks, grassy slopes, sandy beaches and, of course, on the rug in front of our fireplace at home. All such spots offered me ten minutes to get off the Hurry-Flurry Merry-Go-Round and awaken refreshed.

Thomas A. Edison was a famous napper. He made up in the daytime the sleep he missed at night. The famous inventor often slept only four or five hours at night, but is known to have taken as many as six or eight 10-minute naps during his working day. Because of his lifelong hearing impairment, Edison had little trouble dropping off for a few minutes, even in his noisy laboratory. He would then awaken and continue his work.

QUICK RELAXER 2. VISUALIZATION

This method requires a little training, but can be used by nearly everyone after some practice. You use your mind's eye, your imagination, for a quick break. When the pressure's building up, close your eyes and imagine you are at one of your favorite places, parks, or vacation spots.

Visualize that place where you camped last summer. Imagine you can *see* the forest greenery, *smell* the pines, *hear* the birds. *Make* it seem so real that you feel you are actually standing there looking at the lake. You can take a quick "time-out" with the help of your imagination.

Another scene is to visualize yourself in bed early in the morning. You are warm and cozy. Then imagine it's raining and chilly outside. Make yourself *hear* the rain, *feel* the warmth of the bed. Then pretend that you decide to stay in bed another 15 minutes. Thoroughly enjoy the luxury of the situation. Make it happen in your mind.

You'll be amazed at the relief of tension that can result. You can learn to awake from such reveries feeling refreshed.

QUICK RELAXER 3.   FOREHEAD MASSAGE

Another technique you can try when you feel tension building up is to massage your forehead. Close your eyes and use your fingertips to rub in circles and vigorously massage your forehead—then the back of your neck. Rub hard. Rub away the tightness. Remember you have a "First Aid Kit" in your fingertips.

QUICK RELAXER 4.   8-8-8 BREATHER

This method relies on the fact that when people are tense, they breath in a rapid, shallow manner. In order to counteract this tenseness, the 8-8-8 Breather is a useful technique. The exercise has three phases: inhale, hold breath, exhale. It will help to visualize the phases in the triangle shown here:

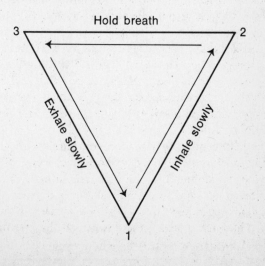

First, gently blow out all the air in your lungs and push out your abdomen, as if you were four months pregnant! *Slowly* count to 8 while inhaling (count "1-and, 2-and, 3-and" to 8). Then hold your breath, again to the count of 8. Finally *slowly* exhale while counting to 8. Breathe normally for a few minutes, then repeat the process. The whole exercise should take two or three minutes. Visualize the triangle in your mind's eye.

The 8-8-8 Breather works surprisingly well. I've used it many times.

QUICK RELAXER 5. ABDOMINAL BREATHER

This relaxer works best if you are lying face up. I do it lying on the floor on a rug. Relax for a few minutes. Now blow out the air in your lungs, and while doing it push out your abdomen as noted above.

Then pull in your "belly" until the front wall of the abdomen seems to touch your spine. Press down on your abdomen with your hand as shown below. Next inhale as deeply as possible.

Press down on your abdomen

Finally relax and let your abdomen return to its normal position. Lie there and breathe normally for a few minutes. Then repeat the whole cycle.

One of the benefits of this Abdominal Breather is that it forces you to breathe deeply. The air we breathe gives us life, yet most of us use only 20 to 30% of our lung capacity. This method helps you use 100% of your capacity.

QUICK RELAXER 6.   GETTING OUT OF A RUT

This surprisingly simple method helps get your mind out of a rut. And if the rut happens to be tension the day you try it, then it becomes Quick Relaxer 6.

There is one simple rule that governs this method: "Make up *new* ways to do *old* things."

1. If you are *right*-handed, wash the dishes, push the vacuum, eat dinner, etc. with your *left* hand—or try writing a letter with the opposite hand.

2. Walk backwards or sideways instead of forward.

3. Add a dance or new movement to your walking, or try my favorite—skipping while you are on a walk.

4. Walk up the steps at your office, home, or factory backwards.

QUICK RELAXER 7.   THE BATHROOM SINGER

People in all walks of life have found that there's more to singing in the bathtub or shower than meets the ears. Loud singing necessitates deep abdominal breathing, which relaxes the singer. Hold your favorite notes for a long time. This, in combination with the heat of the shower or bath water, provides a generally relaxing experience—for even the most keyed-up person—after one of "those days."

I also sing at the top of my voice when I'm in my car on the way to work or to a meeting if I find I'm tensing up. It may "sound" silly, but the sounds work!

QUICK RELAXER 8.   YOUR HOBBIES

If you have a hobby in which you can completely wrap yourself up for a few minutes—listening to music, working on a boat model, examining stamps, making pottery, painting, knitting, or other handwork —you have Quick Relaxer 8.

Such a hobby, where you are in complete control, gives you relaxation. As far as hobbies are concerned, remember Sehnert's Law, "What's fun to do, is good for you."

QUICK RELAXER 9.   STRETCH AWAY TENSION

There are several ways to stretch away tension. Here is one you can start with:

1. Standing upright, put your arms behind your back, twist to the left side while inhaling and stretch. Then twist to the right while exhaling and stretch.

2. Then put your hands together behind your back over your head and bend forward while inhaling deeply and stretch over as far as you can.

3. Now reverse the direction and while exhaling,

1   2   3

bend backwards as far as you can, with your arms outstretched behind your back.

The whole process of stretching while breathing deeply relaxes and refreshes. Deep breathing is important in the stretchers. As you breathe, imagine you are filling yourself up like a balloon.

QUICK RELAXER 10.   RELAXATION RESPONSE

Herbert Benson, M.D., of Harvard University, developed the "relaxation response." After he compared transcendental meditation, Zen, yoga, autogenic training, progressive relaxation, hypnosis with suggested deep relaxation, and several other self-regulation techniques, he observed that they all had four basic elements in common:

1. Quiet environment
2. Mental device such as a sound or word
3. Passive attitude to help one rest and relax
4. Comfortable position to reduce muscular effort to a minimum

From these elements he created the method that has been described in his best-selling book, *Relaxation Response*.

1. In a quiet environment, sit in a comfortable position.
2. Close your eyes.
3. Relax all your muscles, beginning with your feet and progressing to calves, thighs, lower torso, chest, shoulders, neck, head. Allow them to remain deeply relaxed.
4. Breathe through your nose. Become aware of your breathing. Say the word *one* silently to yourself as you breathe in; repeat it when you breathe out.
5. Continue this practice for 20 minutes. You may open your eyes to check the time, but do not use an alarm clock. When you finish, sit quietly for several more minutes, at first with your eyes closed, then later with your eyes open.

Don't worry about whether you are successful in achieving a deep level of relaxation. You should maintain a passive attitude and let relaxation occur at its own pace. If distracting thoughts occur, ignore them and repeat the word "one."

The relaxation response should be practiced once or twice daily but not within two hours after a meal, since the digestive process interferes with the process of relaxation.

These 10 Quick Relaxers will help you counter the fight-or-flight response involved in the development of stress-related diseases. They will help you get off the Hurry-Flurry Merry-Go-Round. They will help you maintain the equilibrium of the autonomic nervous system. They help you, in the words of Dr. Ken Dychtwald, author of *Body Mind,* "focus on the body in such a way that the mind becomes quiet and clear. Just as stress and unwellness in the body can generate confusion in the mind, stillness in the body can help produce a deep state of peace of mind."

15

Unstress Exercises

The use of deep breathing and stretching to relax is instinctive to all of us. We've all had these experiences:

- You've finished a difficult, two-hour examination at school.
- You've arrived home after driving your car through heavy traffic.
- You've sat through an intense and important three-hour meeting.

You feel tired, tense, irritable. You really need to unwind, to relax. You instinctively yawn and stretch your arms and body. You can then begin to relax and unwind.

The deep breathing and stretching helped you to relax (which means to make less tense, to loosen, to grow milder) and to *unwind* (which means to loosen from a coiled condition, to disengage).

The Unstress Exercises in this chapter have been designed to help you relax and unwind in a similar natural way. They are planned to help you stretch your muscles and improve the mobility of your joints in your arms, hands, legs, feet, and spine and teach you to breathe deeply and slowly.

You may even receive a bonus or two beyond relaxation, as I did. I injured my back when I was in the Navy in World War II. For many years afterward I was troubled with chronic backaches. The exercises I will tell you about helped increase my spine's flexibility, got rid of my backaches, and probably kept me away from the neurosurgeons. The exercises are now part of my daily exercise ritual—and when I skip them for a few days, my backaches return to remind me of my folly.

Mobility of your spine is especially important. The spine is the only joint system in the body that can move in five directions. It can bend (1) left, (2) right, (3) forward, (4) backward, and (5) twist like a corkscrew. As I noted in How to Be Your Own Doctor (Sometimes), "By our 20th birthday, most of us had stopped using the spine except to bend forward to tie our shoelaces." When we add to the problem by sitting all day, first humped over the steering wheel of a car on the way to work, then hunched over a desk, bench, or typewriter at our job, and finally hunkered down in a chair or davenport in front of the TV set, it's no wonder our spine objects by giving us backaches. When we lose the flexibility of our spine, then abuse it by poor sitting and working habits, backaches begin.

SIX BASIC UNSTRESS EXERCISES

Here is my exercise ritual:

1. Find a time in the day, preferably at night, when there are no other distractions such as phones, visitors, or family interruptions.

2. Set up a procedure that is almost a ritual. Do it the *same* way every night.

3. Wear comfortable, loose-fitting pajamas or leotards while exercising. (Do each exercise five times, but for beginners two or three times are enough.)

4. Spread a large beach towel on a carpeted area (or a comforter or heavy blanket on a hard floor). Use the same room every night.

5. Keep the lights in the room subdued and turn off radio and television.

6. Do the exercises in a specific sequence: (1) Corpse (for relaxation), (2) Breathing Posture, (3) Leg Stretch, (4) Cobra, (5) Shoulder Stand, and (6) Spinal twist, as shown in the following diagrams:

1. Corpse

1. Lie as flat as possible on your back with arms out at your sides, palms up.

2. Breathe deeply and concentrate on relaxing your entire body starting with toes and working up.

Corpse and Breathing Posture

2. Breathing Posture

1. Lie flat on back with arms at sides.

2. Take a slow, deep breath and raise both arms

145

above your head. Push your abdomen out as you inhale and fill your entire chest with air. Stretch your
body as tall as possible.

3. Hold your breath as long as possible and then exhale *slowly* through your nose as you lower arms to
your sides. Pull abdomen in as you exhale.

3. Leg Stretch

1. Lie flat on back with arms at sides.

2. Raise right leg as high as you comfortably can
with knee straight.

3. Slowly lower leg to floor, tightening your buttocks as you do so.

4. Repeat procedure with left leg.

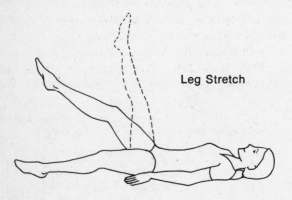

Leg Stretch

4. Cobra

1. Lie face down on floor.

2. Place hands next to chest.

3. Keep elbows bent and close to body.

4. Slowly raise head from floor and bend head and
neck back as far as possible.

5. Now raise shoulders; keep palms on floor and elbows bent.

6. Slowly lower body to the floor.

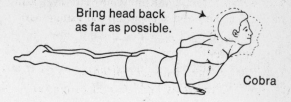

Bring head back as far as possible.

Cobra

5. Shoulder Stand

1. Lie flat on back.

2. Elevate both legs over head (as if "bicycling").

3. Support hips with hands, elbows taking weight, and get up as high on shoulders and neck as possible. Keep body straight, chin pressed into neck.

4. Hold position for three to five minutes.

5. Slowly lower legs and back to floor. Uncurl vertebra by vertebra.

Shoulder Stand

6. Spinal twist

1. Sit with right leg partly extended and left knee

flexed with left foot close in to right buttock. Grab right knee with left arm.

2. Twist body and place outstretched right arm behind you to right. Reach as far as you can behind you and look over right shoulder in twisting motion.

3. Repeat the twist in *opposite* direction with *left* leg extended, right knee flexed, and right foot close in to left buttock.

4. This is a difficult position, so go slowly. It takes some people a long time to master it.

Spinal Twist

When doing the above exercises, remember that each should be accompanied by slow, deep breathing —deeply inhale with the beginning of the position, hold the breath and slowly exhale at completion. Work out your patterns.

The entire sequence should take about 30 minutes. Add your variations to the exercises as you increase your flexibility and skills. At the completion of the sequence you will feel refreshed and relaxed.

FIVE EXTRA EXERCISES FOR LATER USE

In addition to these there are several other exercises

that you might want to add. It took me about a year before I did them with comfort, so start with the Six Basic Unstress Exercises before you expand your skills to these:

Knee-chest

1. Lie flat on back with arms at sides.
2. Bend knees and bring heels back to touch buttocks.
3. Wrap your arms around legs, pulling them close to your chest.
4. Keep head on the floor and continue gentle squeezing of your legs while flattening spine against the floor.

(*Note:* In this position some will feel a clicking sensation as the vertebra align themselves. This is a normal occurrence.)

Cat Stretch

1. Kneel on hands and knees. Back straight, parallel to floor with arms and legs like a table, palms flat.
2. While inhaling, arch your back, pull in your buttocks, and bring your head toward your chest. Hold for three seconds.
3. While exhaling, bend your back, expand your chest and raise your head as far as possible. Hold for three seconds.
4. Relax and repeat sequence three times.

Variation of Cat Stretch

1. Kneel on hands and knees as in first position.
2. While inhaling, bend the right knee, lower your head and bring your knee to your forehead. Hold for three seconds.

3. While exhaling, extend your leg, expand your chest and raise your head as far back as possible. Feel the stretch along your leg, back and neck. Hold for three seconds.
4. Repeat with left leg.
5. Repeat sequence three times.

Knee and Thigh Stretch
1. Sit on the floor with legs apart and outstretched.
2. Grasp your left ankle with left hand and right ankle with right hand.
3. Bring your heels up to your buttocks.
4. Put your arms on inner surface of knees, grasp feet, and while exerting pressure on your knees with your elbows, pull your feet towards your body.
5. Bend your head and shoulders and try to touch your feet with your head.
6. Repeat several times.

Forward Bend
1. Sit on the floor with legs together and out-stretched.
2. Inhale, raise your arms over head, stretch, exhale.
3. Bend forward with forehead to your knees to maximum stretch. Do not overextend.
4. Relax your neck and shoulders and place hands on legs where you can reach.
5. Breathe evenly and hold as long as the position is comfortable.

In addition to the benefits of relaxation you receive from the Unstress Exercises that have been outlined, some recent scientific and medical applications have been discovered:
1. Recent studies show that the spine bending not

only helps keep the fibrous tissue between the bony vertebrae more flexible but such movement apparently squeezes nearby vascular tissue and helps bring vital nourishment to the intervertebral discs, those pads between each vertebra as shown below:

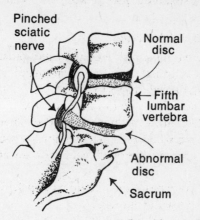

The discs that thus retain a healthier flexibility are less likely to deteriorate through normal use, or, if injured, they should repair more promptly.

2. Senior citizens I studied while I was at Georgetown University learned to use a prebedtime ritual that included these Unstress Exercises. These older Americans were able to relax and sleep normally without relying on over-the-counter and prescription products for sleep as they had before the study.

3. Patients who have high blood pressure are able to cut down on the amount of antihypertensive medication they need each day—and in some cases stop it altogether—when they use a combination of vigorous regular exercises such as jogging, biking, or walking and similar unstress exercises on a daily basis.

4. People who experience high levels of nervous

tension that can result from a hurry-flurry life-style, can break the cycle of events that lead to increased pulse rates and elevated blood pressure. The cycle can be broken by using unstress exercises during lunch hour or at stressful times during the day, by relaxing themselves. This, in turn, brings their autonomic nervous system back to neutral position.

Autonomic Nervous System

Sympathetics overactivated	Parasympathetics activated	Neutral balance

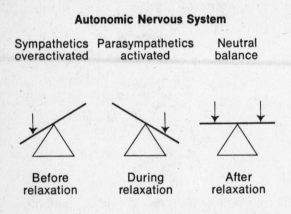

Before relaxation	During relaxation	After relaxation

5. The shoulder stand with the individual's feet thrust toward the ceiling provides a welcome relief to the blood vessels (which must retain a tensed condition all day long while you stand and sit) and improves the circulation of the legs. At the same time it tips the tables on the vessels of your head and neck. This change in their vascular tone helps blow out the cobwebs—and often the "blahs"—in your mind, leaving you feeling refreshed.

The Six Basic Unstress Exercises, plus the five extra I've described, provide benefits that are well worth the 30 minutes you invest in them at the end of each day. Because of the help they provide, many people even practice an abbreviated version of them at noon.

To all of us they offer a natural, safe, quick and inexpensive way to relax and unwind. Most of us will gain improved looks through better posture and the refreshing look that follows good sleep. Others, like myself, gain freedom from chronic backaches. Still others are able to relieve tension without resorting to alcohol or tranquilizers.

All in all, the methods described are some of the best of the Unstress Remedies. They set the stage for Way No. 4: Take Care of Your Body.

16

Nutrition and the Seven Golden Rules for Good Health

I know my friend, Dr. Lester Breslow, former dean of the U.C.L.A. School of Public Health, will be pleased when he reads this chapter. I consider the work he did with the help of his colleague, Nedra Belloc, in identifying the seven most common personal health practices, as one of the most significant medical studies of this century.

The health practices described by Breslow and Belloc in *Preventive Medicine* (9, 469-483, 1980) were:

1. Never smoking cigarettes.
2. Moderate or no use of alcohol.
3. Getting regular physical activity.
4. Obtaining 7-8 hours sleep/day regularly.
5. Maintaining proper weight.
6. Eating breakfast.
7. Not eating between meals.

These practices involve a wide range of activities.

The last three are directly correlated and two others are closely linked with nutritional habits.

When the original study on 6928 adults in Alameda County, California was made in 1965 and then followed up in 1974, medical scientists like myself had some hunches they were important, but didn't know why. As a boy my mom had always told me, "Keith, it's important to eat your breakfast." As I grew older, I knew that my neighbors who were on the slender side—but not too skinny—often lived longer than their overweight neighbors. I had observed that persons who did vigorous work, like the farmers and carpenters in the Midwestern towns I lived in, seemed to live longer. It also seemed apparent that smoking and abuse of alcohol usually brought earlier disease and death. But it took the work of Belloc and Breslow and later collaborators, such as James E. Eustrom, Lisa Berkman, and S. Leonard Syme, to nail down all these important facts:

- The physical health status of persons who followed seven good health practices was consistently about the same as persons *30 years younger* who followed few or none of these practices.
- The association of these seven health habits with physical health status was independent of age, sex, and income level.
- Persons who practice good health habits and maintain close social relationships through (1) marriage, (2) contacts with close friends and relatives, (3) church membership, and (4) informal and formal group associations were the healthiest individuals in the studies.

In other words, the person who has the shortest life expectancy would be like my bachelor cousin, Archie, who:

- Gets up at 6:00 a.m. feeling so hungover he often skips breakfast at 7:00 (except for two cups of coffee and two cigarettes) so he can get to work at 8:00.

- Eats a heavy lunch at noon at the office cafeteria and later buys snacks (mostly so-called "junk" foods) from the vending machine.
- Seldom does more exercise than walk from his car in the parking lot to his place of work.
- Has a 50-inch waist to go along with his 200+ pounds.
- Frequently consumes five cans of beer per night while watching TV or playing poker with his pals.
- Manages to smoke two packs of cigarettes per day.
- To his credit he manages to get 7-8 hours of sleep (otherwise his score would be 0 out of 7).

Those who know Archie also know he hasn't been to church for 40 years and thinks social clubs and civic organizations—except his American Legion Club —are a "lot of bunk." Archie, once a trim Marine, is only 50, but looks over 60 and has a cardiovascular age of more like 70. Needless to say, Archie feels rotten much of the time.

On the other side of the coin is my friend, Caroline. She is an attractive 50-year-old who looks 40 and acts 30. Her day goes like this:

- Gets her eight hours of sleep and rises feeling refreshed.
- Goes to a nearby park to jog ½ mile at 7:00 and often adds a vigorous bike ride at 5 P.M. when she gets home from work.
- Has a good breakfast in a leisurely manner now that the children are all off at college.
- Has a light nutritious lunch before she goes to her afternoon job as a bookkeeper and business manager of a small company.
- Doesn't smoke.

Caroline, our Wellness Winner, practices unstress exercises most evenings before bedtime. She regularly attends services at her church, where she is an active volunteer.

Caroline keeps in touch with friends through her civic club and college sorority and maintains a warm family relationship with her brother, sister, and parents. When old friends see her, they say Caroline has as much energy and good looks as her college-age daughters—and she does!

What will Caroline—and others who maintain good health—find out about the benefits of this positive life-style when she is subjected to a stressful life situation such as death of a spouse or other traumatic event, or serious injury or illness of herself or in the family? My experience over the past 25 years as a physician is that she will come through just fine—as you will, too, if you practice all or most of the Seven Rules. You and Caroline can be bruised by the vicissitudes of life and its inevitable losses, but your health will help you withstand them in better shape.

Archie, on the other hand, has such a shallow "Well of Health" to call upon that for him personal loss and turmoil can quickly lead to big trouble—trouble that has been lurking in the background for years. Such a "last straw" for Cousin Archie occurred following a relatively minor traffic accident. One night Archie backed his car out of the Legion Club parking lot and hit a truck. In the altercation that followed, Archie's exertion—and anger—caused him to keel over in the parking lot with a near-fatal heart attack.

When it comes to self-care and stress management, we can see by the stories of Archie and Caroline that what people *eat*, and *drink*, and *smoke*, and *do* with themselves on a regular basis make a great deal of difference in how they respond to the turbulences of life.

THE CONTROVERSY OVER NUTRITION

Caroline told me recently that as she developed

her healthy way of life, her biggest problem was in her eating habits. She had difficulty in fitting together the conflicting advice she received regarding nutrition. The articles and books she reads compare processed sugar vs. raw sugar, natural vitamins vs. man-made, and "artificial this" vs. "100% organic that." One article states that sugar is bad, while another proclaims it an essential nutrient. One expert says you need fat, while an equally eminent one says you don't. A TV ad proclaims, "You all need trace minerals," while a week later an article says, "We don't know which trace minerals are essential." Caroline read Adelle Davis' books, which told readers that if they followed her dietary advice they wouldn't get cancer—yet Caroline read that Davis herself died of cancer. Articles in *Prevention* magazine advocated megadoses of vitamins, while *Consumer Reports* said the articles were deceptive and biased toward the advertisers who spend $2 million per month with *Prevention*.

"Who can I believe?" Caroline wondered.

In the whole nutrition scene, a few things, though, seemed to make sense to Caroline. She had no trouble accepting the facts that she and most Americans exercised too little, ate too much salt, too many calories in general and too many sweets in particular. She adjusted her diet and that of the family accordingly. She followed the guidelines established by the U.S. Department of Health and Human Services and the Department of Agriculture:

1. Eat a variety of foods
2. Maintain ideal weight
3. Avoid too much fat, saturated fat, and cholesterol
4. Eat foods with adequate starch and fiber
5. Avoid too much sugar
6. Avoid too much sodium
7. If you drink alcohol, do so in moderation

Another way of describing these dietary goals and what they meant to Caroline and to the average American is shown in this chart.

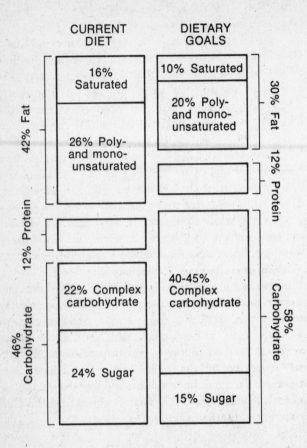

CURRENT DIET

DIETARY GOALS

42% Fat
- 16% Saturated
- 26% Poly- and mono-unsaturated

12% Protein

46% Carbohydrate
- 22% Complex carbohydrate
- 24% Sugar

30% Fat
- 10% Saturated
- 20% Poly- and mono-unsaturated

12% Protein

58% Carbohydrate
- 40-45% Complex carbohydrate
- 15% Sugar

Some personal beliefs about nutrition were provided by Dr. C. Norman Shealy, Director of the Pain and Health Rehabilitation Center in LaCrosse, Wisconsin. Shealy, author of *90 Days to Self-Health,* is a neurosurgeon-turned-holistic-medicine practitioner. In an article, "Stress Is More Than Emotions," he alleged this about stress, our life-styles, and their effects on nutritional needs:

All demands which exceed eustress lead to at least one common biochemical reaction—an increase in blood sugar followed by release of insulin. If the blood sugar then falls rapidly (over 30 mg% in 30 minutes or below 70 mg%), this in itself becomes a stressor with release of ACTH and serotonin, cortisone and norepinephrine, increase in blood sugar, release of insulin, and the potentially vicious cycle starts again.

Modern Americans consume two and a half pounds of processed sugar per person per *week*. This accounts for about 25% of all calories—and these are totally lacking in the vitamins and minerals needed to metabolize sugar. Furthermore, the sugar is rapidly absorbed, leads to overstimulation of insulin and eventually to exhaustion of the pancreas—part of the end-stage of Selye's General Adaptation Syndrome. By contrast Westerners 150 years ago ate only about two pounds of sugar per *year*—an increase of over 75 times. Excess sugar depletes the individual of vitamins, tryptophan, potassium, zinc, chromium, manganese and lithium, and favors a reaction which forces calcium and manganesium into the soft tissues. It also alters blood lipids in an undesirable way, inhibits the immune mechanism, and is an unreasonable demand upon the body.

Shealy has this to say about cigarettes, coffee, and alcohol:

Nicotine is a powerful stimulus to the stress reaction as is caffeine, and the two together have a geometrically progressive effect. Thus the worst imaginable breakfast, much worse than fasting, consists of a cup of coffee with cream and sugar, a sweet roll, and a cigarette. Alcohol is in its simplest effect not much different from sugar. Although it does "relax" emotional nervousness temporarily, pure mental techniques for relaxation are far less costly and healthier.

161

THE CONTROVERSY OVER VITAMIN C

Then there was the whole controversy about Dr. Linus Pauling and vitamin C. What was vitamin C's role in preventing and treating the common cold? Was it useful in preventing cancer and hardening of the arteries? Caroline often asked herself, "Who is right?"

The controversy surrounding Pauling and vitamin C still rages on. In his book *Vitamin C, the Common Cold and the Flu,* Pauling claimed that persons taking 1000 mg. (roughly 20 times the Recommended Daily Allowance) of vitamin C daily would have 45% fewer colds and suffer 60% fewer days of illness.

That started a debate which has continued for much of the last decade. Many creditable scientists doubted Pauling's claims and noted that megadoses of vitamin C gave susceptible persons kidney stones or gallstones, neutralized some drugs a doctor might prescribe, falsified the result of laboratory tests that diabetics use to check their urine for sugar, and re-geared the body's metabolism to require these high doses (with the related danger that when the person stopped vitamin C "cold turkey," it would plunge the person into severe C depletion, which in the case of pregnant women could produce "rebound scurvy" in their newborn babies).

Pauling countered with claims that vitamin C is among the least toxic substances known. He alleged that taking high doses of C is "probably less danger-ous than drinking the tap water of most large cities!"

Pauling, a two-time Nobel Prize winner, asserted that virtually every living thing manufactures its own supply of vitamin C from simple sugars—except guinea pigs, apes, and human beings. This defect, he theo-rizes, is the result of a genetic accident in human development. He claimed that when sick, injured, or otherwise under stress, people need even more C to help the healing process.

One of Pauling's skeptics, Dr. Terence W. Anderson, then at the University of Toronto, was initially so outraged by the claims that he set out to disprove them. He started studies in the winter of 1971-72. When the sophisticated tests were over, he reported: "Pauling was half right about vitamin C and colds. It prevented few colds but was a powerful help in reducing the severity." Anderson more recently found megadoses no better than 200 mg. and concluded, "We should adhere to the principle of 'first do no harm' and advise the public to limit their daily intake to 100 or 200 mg."

Dr. Victor Herbert, a respected scientist and nutrition specialist from the Bronx, N.Y., Veteran's Administration Medical Center, notes in *Nutrition Cultism: Facts and Fiction:* "It has been alleged that vitamin C prevents colds. As it happens, there is absolutely no evidence for that. . . . There is some slight evidence that it may have a mild antihistaminic effect. If we take that claim at its most favorable possibility, is it worthwhile to take a megadose of C 365 days a year, with possible undesirable side effects, in order to achieve a mild antihistamine effect during the eight days of the entire year that the average person has a cold?"

Studies have shown that when viruses attack our body, as in the common cold, normal amounts of vitamin C help form the collagen "glue" between the cells of the membranes of the nose and throat. In some experimental situations, C may also help produce an antiviral chemical, interferon, create more white blood cell lymphocyctes, immunogloblens, and prostaglandins—all key elements in our immunity system—and aid in the repair of our adrenal glands and help make adrenaline and other hormones, but none of this has been demonstrated in the living human.

The hard question, "How much vitamin C is enough?" however, has still not been answered. The Recommended Daily Allowance is 60 mg. day for an average adult, 80 mg. for pregnant women, and 100 mg. for a nursing mother. Pauling says that the R.D.A. dose is only enough C to prevent scurvy, not enough for optimal health. He sticks by his 1000 mg. per day for maintenance and 4000 mg. per day when coming down with a cold or flu. Dr. Anderson, now at the University of British Columbia, recommends 100 to 150 mg. on normal days and 500 milligrams during the first days of a cold or when under stress.

AN ADDITIVE PROCESS

My experience—and that of Shealy's—has been that the effects of faulty life-styles and nutritional habits are additive.

Additive Stressors

Chemical:	Sugar, caffeine, nicotine, alcohol, salt (over 2 gm/day), DDT and chemical poisons, smog
Physical:	Inactivity, trauma/accidents, weather, infectious agents (viruses and bacteria), excess work (if in poor level of physical fitness)
Emotional:	Fear, anger, depression, guilt, anxiety

The total biochemical reaction of each individual—such as that which has affected Cousin Archie over the years—results from the interaction of all nutritional, physical environment, and social demands—and how we practice, or don't practice, the Seven Rules.

On the other side of the ledger unstress activities

are also additive. Good nutrition plus relaxation and recreation equal good health.

ADDITIVE UNSTRESSORS

Avoiding Bad Habits:	Sweets, caffeine, smoking, alcohol
Physical Exercise:	Limbering of joints, muscles, tendons; strengthening with aerobic exercises
Relaxation/Self Regulation:	Relaxation with unstress exercises, meditation, autogenic training, prayer

THE SEVEN RULES FOR GOOD HEALTH

To summarize this chapter, let's look in more detail at the Seven Golden Rules for Good Health.

Rule 1. Never smoke cigarettes. Nicotine is present in all tobacco and is a stimulant. Nicotine increases the pulse rate and the blood pressure—responses that are already in overdrive when your body is reacting to the "fight or flight syndrome." Therefore, "smoking to relax" while under stressful conditions is a misconception. Instead of helping, it actually exaggerates the problem.

Rule 2. Avoid alcohol or use it moderately. Alcohol is the oldest and most widely used tranquilizer. Millions of people use it as their solution to being tense or emotionally upset. Ten percent of the entire population in the U.S. abuse alcohol to the point that it is a major factor in divorce, business productivity, accidents, and illness. Alcohol has no useful role in stress management.

Rule 3. Get regular physical activity. Regular exercise and vigorous work are essential in the healthy control of stress. It is also important in maintaining control of your weight and enhancing restful sleep.

Rule 4. Obtain 7-8 hours sleep each day regularly. Sleep refreshes and rebuilds us. It restores the balance between the sympathetic and parasympathetic nervous systems. Disturbed sleep is often the first signal that your body gives you regarding stress overload and the way you are handling stressful situations in your family or job.

Rule 5. Maintain proper weight. The weight persons maintain is an important index of how well they are managing their total health. Overweight itself is not now thought of as a specific health hazard, but it helps set the stage for many problems. Food is used as a tranquilizer for many people, and a sudden increase in weight of 10-15 pounds can serve as a red light that indicates you are in a stressful situation.

What is your proper weight? There are scores of tables that have been prepared that are based on variables such as sex, bone size, and age of the individual. One table might show you to be "overweight" while another rates you as "ideal." The best way to calculate your weight is the Ideal Weight Formula:

Female: 100 + 5 pounds for each 1″ above 60″ = ___
Male: 106 + 6 pounds for each 1″ above 60″ = ___

(1) Your weight is that without shoes and undressed.

(2) If your weight is 20% above that number, you are enough overweight to start losing excess poundage. This is especially true if you are suffering from diabetes, hypertension, coronary disease, gall bladder disease, or arthritis in weight-bearing joints.

Example:

1. Carolyn weighs 115 pounds and is 5′ 6″ (66 inches). Ideal Weight Formula for Females: 100 + 30 (5 x 6) = 130 pounds. Carolyn is on the slender side of the calculated weight, and, as a matter of record, weighs what she did when she graduated from high school.

2. Archie weighs 220 pounds and is 5′ 11″ (71 inches). Ideal Weight Formula for Males: 106 + 66 (6 x 11) = 172 pounds. Archie is 22% overweight. He weighed 170 pounds when he joined the U. S. Marine Corps in 1945.

Ideally you should be on the slender side of the weight you calculated—which for most adults is also the weight they held when they graduated from high school, started college, or went into the military service. However, "moderation in all things" also holds for slenderness. Dr. Reubin Andres of Johns Hopkins University reviewed 16 studies in the U.S. and around the world that suggest being *underweight* can be as risky as being *overweight*.

Rule 6. Eat breakfast. Our mothers and grandmothers have always told us, "You must eat breakfast." When you awaken in the morning, you have been fasting for 10 to 12 hours and need fuel to start the day. Even though you have been sleeping for seven or eight of those hours, you have been burning up stored fuel. Studies of basal metabolic rates (BMR)—the energy needed to keep your body warm and functioning at a basal level—show that persons burn up ⅔ of their food keeping the "vital juices" flowing. The other ⅓ calories taken in are used to give the energy required for work and exercise activities. Therefore, the advice given by your mother makes good sense.

It makes even more sense when you start your day with a breakfast that includes the Basic Four Food Groups:

1. *Fruit-Vegetable Group*—dark green and yellow vegetables, tomatoes, potatoes, fruits
2. *Grain Group*—cereals, breads, macaroni, whole grain products
3. *Animal/Vegetable Protein Group*—eggs, meat, fish, poultry, beans, peas, nuts

4. *Milk-Dairy Product Group*—cheese, yogurt, ice cream, milk

A good breakfast would, for example, include a half of a grapefruit or orange juice, toast or cereal, cheese or meat, and milk or cocoa.

Rule 7. Don't snack between meals. If you interpret this to mean, as I do, "three square meals a day and no snacks between meals," what is a "square meal"? It is one that includes servings from the Basic Four. The number of servings you need from each group during breakfast and the rest of the meals during the day varies, depending on your age.

1. *Fruit-Vegetable*—4 servings
2. *Grain*—4 servings
3. *Animal/Vegetable Proteins*—2 servings
4. *Milk-Dairy Products*—2 servings adult, 3 servings children, 4 servings teen-agers

The danger of eating between meals is that snacking alters the normal ebb and flow of blood sugar that is vitally important in your metabolism of food. Located in your brain is an appetite control center, called the appestat, which responds to blood-sugar levels. A normal level registers 100 mg.% blood glucose. When you are active—working, walking, and so on—you "burn up" the glucose (sugar), and the level will drop to 75 or 80 mg.%. This drop triggers the appestat (much like a drop in temperature triggers the thermostat in your home, which in turn ignites your furnace) and "turns on" hunger feelings. This causes you to eat, and the blood glucose level rises to 115 or 120 mg.%, and this "shuts off" the hunger feelings. The human body loves a routine, including an eating routine, and unhealthy life-style habits can seriously alter this important balance of nature.

So snacks have a multiple danger. They not only

add unnecessary calories but also alter the delicate ebb and flow related to metabolism, digestion, and activity, designed to give you the exact amount of nutrients required to balance your basal metabolic and activity needs.

Eating "three squares" per day balanced with food from the Basic Four makes snacking less likely. Occasional snacks are all right, but they should be nutritious foods such as fruit (both fresh and dried), juices, nuts, and fresh vegetables. Sometimes the "hungries" can be controlled by a brisk walk around the block or vigorous indoor exercises.

The Seven Golden Rules of Good Health do make a difference in how you respond to stressful events. How do you rate with them? When you are in high pressure situations and usually score *yes* in five or six of the Seven Rules—you'll usually do all right. If not—watch out!

17

Exercise:
Your Safest Tranquilizer

In one issue of the *Wall Street Journal* I saw these articles:

- *Time* magazine announced it is paying $400 of the $500 fee for all their employees over 35 years of age who signed up for jogging exercise at New York's Cardio-Fitness Center.

- Deseret Pharmaceuticals, Inc. reported it had installed six exercise bicycles and strategically placed them throughout its Sandy, Utah, headquarters for use by its 1000 employees.

- Officials at Pepsi Cola Corporation reported they had finished arrangements to have jogging tracks, courts for basketball, tennis, and volleyball, a football field, and a baseball diamond at their headquarters in Purchase, New York.

- From San Francisco there was an article about the Public Advocate's office, telling how six lawyers and 25 clerks run each day.

- Seattle sources reported on an ambitious exercise program for employees at the Puget Sound Power and Light Company.

ACROSS OUR NATION

Exercise is setting a trend. A walk through your local library or favorite bookstore provides overwhelming evidence that exercise is—if you'll pardon the pun—off and running in America. Here are a few of the books I saw one day:

- Cooper, Kenneth H., *The Aerobic Way*
- Katch, Frank I., McArdle, W. B. and Boylan, B. R., *Getting in Shape*
- Higdon, Hal, *Fitness Over Forty*
- Fixx, James F., *The Complete Book of Running*

We all know friends, fellow workers, and neighbors who give personal testimonials about exercise like these:

- "It reduces the cholesterol in my blood."
- "If I walk to work each day, I can keep my weight down."
- "I sleep so much better when I work out."
- "It helps my posture and looks."
- "Since I've been running, I've finally quit smoking."
- "As soon as my back starts to ache, it tells me I have to start my exercises again!"

Arthur S. Leon, M.D., an internationally recognized healthsports expert and faculty member at the University of Minnesota's Laboratory of Physiological Hygiene, said that exercise helps through:

    1. Improved cardiovascular efficiency by reducing myocardial oxygen requirements. This results from the reduction in heart rate, and sometimes blood pressure and skeletal muscle adaptations.

    2. Possible increased myocardial vascularity (increased blood supply to the heart muscle).

3. Reduction in body weight and adiposity. This may be associated with reduction in blood lipids (fats), blood pressure, and improved glucose tolerance.

4. Increased cellular sensitivity to insulin, reducing insulin requirements at any glucose level.

5. Reductions in elevated blood triglycerides and VLDL (very low density lipoproteins) and an increase in the amount of cholesterol carried by HDL (high density lipoproteins).

6. Improvement in other health habits including cessation of smoking and better attention to proper diet.

7. Improved stress management

EXERCISE VS. STRESS

It's that last statement, "improved stress management," that I want to discuss further. What is there about exercise that makes it useful for people who want to manage their stress more effectively? Why is a dose of running or brisk walking usually better (and safer) than a dose of tranquilizers?

One of the first documented studies about the mental-health value of exercise was done at the University of Wisconsin. John Greist, a psychiatrist, did a study in 1976 which showed that jogging was a better treatment for depression than psychotherapy. In a pilot study eight clinically depressed patients participated in a 10-week running program. Six of them were cured of their depression. Greist noted that such a "cure rate" of 75 percent was substantially better than the recovery rate for similar patients treated with the traditional psychotherapy he and his staff offered.

In that study the eight patients walked and ran both alone and in groups from two to seven times a week. Most of them recovered from their depression after the first three weeks of the program and maintained their recovery with regular exercise. Patients were interviewed by computer every two weeks. By using this method the data about their health was collected without the injection of a possibly biased human interviewer. In 1978 Dr. Greist and his team of psychiatrists and psychologists expanded the study to another 28 depressed patients and found that for most of them 30 to 45 minutes of jogging three times a week was at least as effective as talk therapy.

Since then other psychiatrists, such as Robert S. Brown of the University of Virginia, Charlottesville, and Ronald M. Lawrence of the University of California in Los Angeles, also found that exercise worked better than pills in controlling depression.

Dr. Lawrence, founder and president of the American Medical Jogger's Association, an organization with more than 3000 members, told *Time* magazine: "Man was meant to be a moving animal, but he's become sedentary. Distance running can bring us back to the basic of what we're here for."

Thaddeus Kostrubala, M.D., a psychiatrist, marathoner, and author of *The Joy of Running*, has developed an unusual method of psychotherapy for his patients. He does psychotherapy while jogging alongside them and has trained "running therapists" to treat depression, drug addiction, and schizophrenia. Kostrubala notes, "I think this is a new and powerful way of reaching the unconscious. . . . I have talked to many runners—runners who run long, medium and short distances—and I have come to the conclusion that running is a form of natural psychotherapy."

Though there is no hard evidence yet, some researchers believe that running cures mental problems by changing chemicals in the body. A Purdue University professor of physical education, A. H. Ismail, recently reported "significant relationships" between changes in hormone levels of joggers and improvements in emotional stability. Skeptics of such reports say that the out-of-shape professors he studied at Purdue felt better simply because they got away from their desks. Ismail still sticks to his theory that exercise produces chemical changes.

Psychiatrist Jerome Katz of the Menninger Foundation in Topeka, Kansas, says that jogging helps make patients more talkative and helps with depression, but commented, "The enthusiastic claims of instant cures of depression have to be evaluated with a great deal of salt."

One nonmedical observer, Clinton Cox of the New York *Daily News*, says about the real secret of such cures, "It's almost impossible to worry about your job or other such mundane pursuits when your body is in total agony!"

Whatever the researchers prove and the skeptics seek to disprove, several things are apparent. Exercise is helpful for many, including me. It blows out mental cobwebs and calms everyday tension. For others it is probably as effective as tranquilizers and alcohol—without the dangers, risks, and side effects. One who agrees with me, Colman McCarthy of *The Washington Post,* reported, "Raising one's pulse focuses the mind more clearly than raising one's glass." McCarthy once suggested that the Senate Finance Committee consider giving tax deductions to those who use their lunch hour for the *two mile run* instead of the *two martini stupor.* McCarthy noted, "Two miles through the park clears the head, restores a sense of identity, relaxes the blood vessels and sends a person back to the office ready to conquer the world—or at least that part of it resting in the in-basket!"

MYTHS ABOUT EXERCISE

Before I propose an exercise plan for you, I want to clear up a few common myths about exercise.

Myth 1. Salt tablets help avoid fatigue. Not true, unless you sweat enough to soak your clothes for an hour or two—as might be the case if you were playing football during practice on a hot day in late August or digging a ditch in the middle of July. Salt tablets can be worse than no salt at all. Salt attracts water and draws it from the tissues, increasing dehydration and the chances of fatigue. Tablets can cause symptoms as they lie on the mucous membrane lining of your stomach and produce enough irritation to make you nauseated. If you expect a vigorous workout, you would be better off to add some extra salt to your food—or eat a handful of salted peanuts.

Myth 2. Put on a sweater immediately after you exercise. Bad advice. Putting on a sweater immediately after you exercise may actually interfere with your body's normal attempts to get rid of heat. The sweater should be put on later when your sweating has subsided and you no longer feel hot. Meanwhile, don't interfere with your body's efforts to cool off and return to its normal temperature.

Myth 3. Don't drink fluids when exercising. Wrong. Replace fluids immediately. Don't wait until you get thirsty. A good rule to follow is to drink a glass of water before you exercise and then replace the fluids with water or juices when exercising as you get dehydrated. Another rule to follow if you are running long distances: "One drink for every five miles of running."

Myth 4. If you can't exercise every day, you better not do it at all. Simply not true. Most experts agree that if you exercise three times weekly with 20 minutes of vigorous aerobic exercise, you will receive cardiovascular benefits.

But remember, the exercise should be vigorous enough to reach your Target Zone, that range when your pulse reaches 70 to 85% of the maximum rate your heart can achieve. This is based on the rate of 220 minus your age, multiplied by 70% or 85%. If you are in good shape, you can safely reach the upper rate; if not, seek the lower rate. For example, if you are 50, and in good shape, the calculation is as follows: 220–50 = 170 x 85% = 144. Your Target Zone is therefore a pulse of 144. If you are not that fit, the rate is 170 x 70% or a 119 pulse rate.

Two notes of caution: (1) Exercise three times weekly but not on consecutive days or weekends only. (2) If you can exercise only once a week, you are advised not to increase your pulse rate to reach the Target Zone.

Myth 5. If you are over 50, just stick to walking. Not necessarily so. Go to any YMCA, YWCA, or athletic club and you'll find active senior citizens working out, running, or swimming. Age alone is not a barrier to exercise. The literature on sports medicine and physical fitness is filled with examples of runners and swimmers who maintain vigorous exercise into their 80s and 90s. There is even the example of one man from California who ran regularly until he was 102! Not only is age no barrier, but handicapping conditions once assumed to be reason for inactivity aren't barriers either. People with a wide variety of neurological, physical, developmental, and mobility problems are now able to take part in many sports. Since 1970 Beitostolen Health Sports Center in Norway has pioneered in helping citizens with disabilities learn healthsports skills. Vinland National Center is being established in Minnesota to help Americans with handicaps learn not only sports skills but also a variety of health, social, and recreational skills. Harold Russell, chairman of the President's Committee on Employment of the Handicapped and a person with a disability himself, has said, "This country is coming around to accept the fact of job equality for handicapped people. But we still have a long way to go for an acceptance of the concept of total well-rounded lives for handicapped people—and that includes more than work, it includes recreation and sports."

WHO SHOULDN'T EXERCISE?

If age and handicap are no barriers to exercise, are there any limits? Yes. The American Medical Association's Committee on Exercise and Physical Fitness said that there are some persons who should not undertake exercise. These are the persons who have the following medical conditions:

- active or recent myocarditis
- recent pulmonary embolism
- congestive heart failure
- arrythmia from third degree A-V block, or if using fixed-rate pacemakers
- aortic aneurysm
- ventricular aneurysm
- liver decompensation
- congenital heart disease, cyanosis

The AMA panel also agreed that any person who has the following medical problems needs a medical history and extensive evaluation by a physician before undertaking an exercise program:

- acute or chronic infectious disease
- diabetes which is not well controlled
- marked obesity
- psychosis or severe neurosis

- central nervous system disease
- musculo-skeletal disease involving spine and lower extremities
- active liver disease
- renal disease with nitrogen retention
- severe anemia
- significant hypertension (diastolic)
- angina pectoris or other signs of myocardial insufficiency
- cardiomegaly
- arrythmia from second degree AV block, ventricular tachycardia, or atrial fibrillation
- significant disease of heart valves or larger blood vessels
- congenital heart disease without cyanosis
- phlebothrombosis or thrombophlebitis
- current use of drugs such as reserpine, propranolol hydrochloride, guanethidine sulfate, guinidine sulfate, nitroglycerin (or other vascular dilators). procainamide hydrochloride, digitalis, catecholamines, ganglionic blocking agents, insulin, or psychotropic drugs.

I won't try to explain what all those conditions are or what the drugs listed do, because I'd need another whole book. The thing to remember, though, is that people who have such conditions or take the drugs noted above represent only 5-10% of the population. Furthermore, these same people will usually know about their problems and recognize what they have—or will seek medical advice if they don't know for sure. If you are apparently healthy and have never been warned by a doctor about such problems, you are a candidate to start conditioning yourself.

One hundred million or more men and women get little or no regular exercise. Among this horde of sedentary Americans are those who never walk when they can ride and who puff as much walking out of a football stadium as the football team does playing on the field. Among that horde will be some who are finding the stresses of life painful enough for them to reconsider their slothful ways. It is to such readers that I recommend my exercise plan. The effort involved will pay dividends in several other ways. It not only will help to relieve stress, it can also help you lose weight, smoke less, sleep better, and feel better.

YOUR EXERCISE PLAN

Step 1. Gear up your body.

One of the easiest ways to gear up is to work exercise into your daily routine. Here are some tips to start:

1. In the morning, get up a half-hour early and take a brisk walk, jog, or bike for 15 minutes before breakfast.

2. When you drive to work or to the grocery store, park in the farthest corner of the lot and walk briskly to and from your car.

3. When you take public transportation, get off the bus or the train several blocks early and walk the rest of the way.

4. If it's a shorter trip, don't take a cab or bus; walk or bike. It's a good habit to develop.

5. At noon, instead of going to the cafeteria or restaurant for lunch, "brown-bag-it" and engage in some sort of exercise program for a half-hour with the time saved.

6. At work take "exercise breaks"—not "coffee breaks"—and walk up and down the stairs, instead of using elevators or escalators.

7. After work, instead of two martinis before dinner, try two laps around the block.

8. If you're bored at home or have time on your

hands, sweep the sidewalk in front of your house or apartment.

9. When you go on an outing to a museum, art gallery, to the beach, or to visit someone, make exercise an essential part of the outing. Try some skipping, tag, Frisbee throwing, or whatever is fun to do with family or friends.

10. During TV commercials run up and down the stairs, do pushups, or jump rope.

11. Do your yard or home chores at a faster rate than normal. As you make the bed, vacuum, sweep, mow, rake, chop wood, shovel snow—speed it up a bit!

12. Turn regular walking into exercise by lifting your heels off the floor, add an extra spring to your step, and while strolling, tense your calf muscles or stretch the hamstrings in your upper legs.

Step 2. Choose your thing.

There are different strokes for different folks. Look at this list and choose something you enjoy doing:

archery	karate
badminton	ping pong
baseball	racquet ball
basketball	rowing
bicycling	(or rowing machine)
bowling	running
canoeing	sailing
fencing	skating
football	skiing (downhill and cross
golf	country)
handball	soccer
hiking	squash
horseback riding	swimming
horseshoe pitching	tennis
jogging	walking
judo	water-skiing
jumping rope	wrestling

Whatever you choose from this list or your own list, find something you *like* to do. I emphasize the word *like* because it's essential that in developing an Exercise Plan you follow Ferguson's Law: "Go for satisfaction, not for accomplishment. Do whatever you need to do to make walking or running (or whatever) fun." There's also another axiom, Sehnert's Law. It has to do with stress management as it relates to exercise, hobbies, and leisure-time activities: "What's fun to do is good for you."

Step 3. Start your plan.

Here are some tips from fitness experts while you are developing your plan. They apply mainly to that most popular exercise of all, running, but are equally applicable to all vigorous exercise programs.

1. *The talk test.* You should be able to talk while you exercise. If you can't, you're working too hard—or running too fast—and should slow down.

2. *Warm up and cool down.* Always do stretching and warm-up exercises before starting and after completing your exercise. Do leg and back stretches, push-ups, and sit-ups.

3. *Don't be intimidated.* Don't let faster runners, better tennis players, or more experienced bikers intimidate you. Do your own thing at your own speed in your own way.

4. *Learn your body's capabilities.* If you are uncoordinated, some competitive sports or activities may be frustrating. If you are tight-jointed and stiff, you may need calisthenics for several weeks before trying such sports or activities.

5. *Learn to take your Resting Pulse.* Because your pulse is needed as a guide to aerobic activity, you should learn to take your pulse at your wrist.

   a. With your hand held palm upward, feel with the first two fingers (index and third) of the other hand at the outside of your wrist near base of your thumb.

b. Then, with the aid of a watch that measures seconds, count the pulse for 30 seconds and multiply by two. The normal resting pulse for adults is 60 to 70—60 beats per minute like the seconds on a clock (for children it will be slightly faster).

6. *Learn your Target Pulse.* In the early stages of training use your target pulse to make sure you aren't exercising too vigorously. The following guidelines can be used and based on the Target Zone described earlier:

- If you are in poor condition, take 150 and subtract your age.

- If you are in fair condition, take 170 and subtract your age.

Step 4. Work at it.

After you have geared up, chosen your exercise, and developed skills, remember that any good exercise should have five characteristics. It should give you a chance to:

Move. One effect of movement such as walking, biking, hiking, jogging is to burn up calories. It has been said of many overweight Americans that it's not that they eat too much, it's that they move too little.

Stretch and breath deeply. Because deep breathing and stretching are known to help relieve tension and help one relax, they should be part of the exercise you choose. Inhale with deep breaths to fill up your lungs and force all the air out when you exhale.

Bend, twist, and swing. Flexibility and agility are components that are as important as muscular endurance and strength. Flexibility refers to the range of movements in the joints. Spinal flexibility is especially important.

Be vigorous and promote aerobic activity. Any exercise you choose should be intense enough to increase your heart rate and make you perspire. It should be sustained for 15-20 minutes to provide the training effect called "aerobic activity." The frequency should be at least three times a week.

Enjoy it. If an exercise program is to be successful, it must be done regularly. To be done regularly, it must be enjoyable. When it's enjoyable, it's relaxing and gives physical, mental, and social benefits. Have fun when you do it.

Set your pace. It may take three or four months of regular training to achieve your Target Pulse. Don't be in a hurry. Some days, your "slow days," you may not feel like doing as much, but that's OK. On "fast days," however, be careful that you don't overdo.

Get good equipment. An essential part of any exercise is good quality equipment and comfortable shoes. The ritual of putting on your exercise togs helps set your mental attitude for the exercise. The process of putting on your jogging suit helps your mind and body get ready.

The human body is the only machine that breaks down when you *don't* use it. You can prevent premature aging and deterioration of muscles and joints by using them with vigorous exercise at least three times per week. Exercise is your safest tranquilizer—and an essential part of your stress-management program.

18

Spiritual Growth Through Prayer

A significant medical development in the past few years is the holistic health movement. Many doctors now realize there are medical reasons, as well as religious ones, for considering the spiritual health of patients. The holistic health concept provides services that link spirit, mind, and body.

Much of the early work in the field came from Granger Westberg, a hospital chaplain who developed the concept, first in Ohio and later in Illinois. Westberg noted that the human body functions *best* when persons receive helping attitudes of love, gratitude, and forgiveness—all spiritual values. The body functions *worst* when attitudes such as hate, anger, and envy are present, and there is a void of spiritual values. He also noted that people with strong spiritual values seemed to weather operations and stressful illnesses more successfully than persons without such resources.

So far, the chapters of *Stress/Unstress* have provided you with self-care tips about creating and maintaining healthy minds and bodies. This is done through better nutrition, regular exercise, unstress remedies, improved surroundings at home and work, and renewal of relationships with family and friends.

This chapter has been developed to help you create and maintain a healthy *spirit*. The advice I offer about prayer and meditation came from my personal experiences and that of others. It is based on medical and theological rationale that I think makes sense.

THE HOLY SPIRIT AT WORK

My own personal experiences are based on the assumption that God has made us stewards not only of the money we make and the land and air we use but also of our body/mind/spirit. I also make the assumption that lay people can and should be not only Activated Patients but also Activated Christians. Such new roles require increased responsibility and action on the part of individuals. Little will happen if individuals maintain traditional passive, dependent roles and assume that someone "out there"—the doctor, the pharmacist, the nurse, the priest, the minister—has the responsibility for their spiritual health.

Too many Christians I know hold to the concept that God is a remote being somewhere "out there" in the distant cosmos. My own conviction has always been that God is present through the Holy Spirit in all creation. I see God in:

- the birth of a baby
- the hands of a surgeon
- the laboratory of a scientist

- the earth of the farmer's field
- the skill of an artist
- the music of a composer
- the souls of ordinary people

I have felt the Holy Spirit at work in myself and in my family. This has been experienced in many small ways over the years and once in a most dramatic way.

The dramatic way came about through the misfortune of one of my daughters, Cynthia, who shortly after her birth developed a serious infection. This led to her becoming profoundly deaf in the first month of her life.

At first my wife and I responded, "Why Cindy?" "Why us?" These are the anguished questions raised by all parents who learn that their child is deaf, retarded, blind, disabled, critically ill, or injured. It is similar to that asked by parents who learn of the death of their offspring in a car accident or military encounter.

Initially, Colleen and I felt feelings of hopelessness and helplessness. We prayed fervently that Cindy would "hear and speak." We felt anger and guilt. We wanted prompt, definitive action from God. When it didn't come over the next year or so, we felt disillusionment.

Then one night, many months and many prayers later, it happened. I had been in Chicago on a business trip and was returning home on the train in a sleeper car. It was a bitterly cold winter night when the train stopped so suddenly at a siding that I was awakened. I pushed up the window shade to see where we were. As I looked out on the snow-covered countryside, I saw a full moon shining behind the crossbars of the railroad crossing. Something forced me to fix my eyes on the sign. Soon the crossing sign became a giant crucifix. I was transfixed by what I saw—and heard. From out of the cross came a brilliant light and a remarkably calm voice that said, "Don't despair. Out of the misfortune of your daughter will come benefits for many." Then the voice and the cross disappeared, and I was left with an experience that changed my attitude about many things.

I am still overcome with emotion when I think of it over 20 years later. What did it mean for me? For my wife? For our daughter?

For Cindy it meant that she eventually did "hear and speak," although with a 95-decibel hearing loss she must "hear" through her skilled lipreading. She can "speak" with a remarkably good voice (considering she has never been able to hear her own voice) and the use of sign language. She has done well as an athlete and a person and is now a college graduate working in recreation and healthsports programs for people with disabilities.

For Colleen and me, it meant that we worked to help Cindy get the best education possible at home and school. It meant thousands of hours of work helping other parents, individuals, and children through the Alexander Graham Bell Association for the Deaf, Sertoma International's Hearing and Speech programs, and the Minnesota Foundation for Better Hearing and Speech. Our efforts, with God's help, have brought "benefits to many" estimated at one time in the tens of thousands. It was a clear example to me of Hans Selye's altruistic egotism. We helped ourselves and our daughter by helping others.

It also started me on the long-term program that I now describe as Productive Prayer, a kind of meditation. It helped me learn to feel the presence of the Holy Spirit. It taught me the meaning of Christ's prayer in the Garden of Gethsemane, "Not as I will, but as thou wilt" (Matt. 26:39).

THE STORY OF KARI

A similar example of meditative prayer is that experienced by Kari. Although Kari told me that running had been important to her in breaking her "hurry-flurry habits," prayer later played an equally important part. When she first took the Self-Test for Stress Levels, she scored nearly 700 points (one of the highest scores I have ever seen). She had gone through marriage, marital separation, personal illness in her family, business readjustment, and change in type of work. Kari found herself circling nearly every other Life Event. In the class where I first met her, I had warned that people with scores of 400 and above have a 90% chance of illness or injury within the next year. I turned out to be a good prophet, because within a few weeks she had the car accident that seriously injured her back and neck.

It was that wreck, plus the wreck of her marriage, that brought Kari to prayer. She recalled later, "I was as demolished as my car. I had fits of depression and I felt I had really botched up my life. I almost lost my mind."

Kari continued, "I prayed constantly, but no help seemed to come. Then at church one Sunday while I was singing, some words came right up off the pages —'Health to the sick in mind, sight to the inly blind.'"

Kari told me her story with tears in her eyes, "I had no sooner had that experience when the pastor read this: 'Come to me, all who labor and are heavy laden, and I will give you rest' (Matt. 11:28).

"It was then that I had the most profound religious experience I've ever known. The Holy Spirit literally jumped into my mind. In a few minutes I felt an overwhelming sense of peace and tranquility. Since then, I've pulled myself together and really worked things out. I look at life differently now. I never let myself get under the gun any more."

"How do you think you've changed most?" I asked.

Kari thought for a few moments and then replied, "I live and think more positively, and I treat others with more respect and consideration than I used to. I try to express my feelings more honestly to others, especially in my relationships with my immediate family and friends."

"What does that mean to you?" I asked her.

"I find myself being a more active Christian. I feel I have a more spiritual attitude about things. I feel like I am connected to some 'underground stream of energy.' I don't know what I feel," said Kari, "but certainly it's a force I never had before!"

MEDICAL AND THEOLOGICAL RATIONALE

I see solid medical rationale for helping people gain a healthier spirit. It helps the whole person improve. In my work in helping people develop plans to lose weight, stop smoking, start jogging, I find that many are disappointed to find out that "will power" alone is often not enough. Old *negative* habits can often be changed only with the addition of new *positive* habits or as a result of changes from the new habits. For example, one overweight man I worked with had been a heavy cigarette smoker for 20 years. He had vowed many times to change. He always failed in the past. He succeeded this time. He found it difficult to smoke while cross-country skiing and also a bother to carry cigarettes. He stopped smoking, lost weight from the exercise, and feels better about himself—all at the same time.

In a similar way, promises to be kinder or be more understanding often don't work. Such changes in behavior traits often can occur only when you feel better about yourself or when you have a more positive relationship with the Holy Spirit. This allows Christ's words and attitudes to become a part of your makeup. Then you gain the qualities of kindness and understanding that you seek.

When you feel better about yourself, your relations with others, and your Christian priorities in life, your chances of success in achieving a healthier body and mind greatly increase. It makes medical good sense to have spiritual growth.

One's spiritual life grows as a result of a whole panorama of religious activities: reading the Bible and devotional materials, listening to religious music, seeing religious works of art, doing acts of charity and good will, participating in formal and informal worship, partaking in various church activities, praying and meditating. Each act of worship, prayer, and meditation contributes to the fabric of spiritual life like individual fibers in a tapestry.

PRODUCTIVE PRAYER

Here is a method that has helped me. I use it to supplement my traditional habits of worship and prayer, and it has led to the concept I call Productive Prayer. This, plus the use of my Secret Seven, I predict will lead to spiritual growth for you.

1. Find quiet time. Choose a time of day that is quiet. There should be no phones, no radios, and no television. I use the hour before bedtime, which in our home is about 11:30 P.M. In this frenetic world of ours, finding a quiet time without family or outside interruptions may be difficult except during the early day or late night hours. I do the exercises and prayer in our bedroom.

2. Get ready. To prepare my body and relax my muscles I use a series of unstress exercises (see Chapter 15). After 10-15 minutes of stretching and slow deep breathing, I am usually ready to begin. Controlled breathing is an important part of the process of preparation. Expiration, the breathing-out phase, is timed to be *twice as long* as the inhalation phase. This kind of breathing has a tranquilizing effect.

3. Take a relaxed position. I then assume a position with my knees on the floor and bowing at the waist, put my forehead on the floor. By this time my body is relaxed and my mind clear. If I am still tired or tense about some personal problem, I may do a few more exercises.

4. Pray. I start by repeating three or four times the phrase, "Dear Father in heaven . . ." I will then aim at personal or family problems or concerns; "How will I keep my Christian priorities?" "Which way will I turn?" "What is the answer to the problem?" "What can I do to help?" I may offer prayers of intercession, thanks, or celebration during the five-to-ten minute interval that follows. I often feel the presence of the Holy Spirit during the prayers.

5. Finish the exercises. I then finish the series I've started in a ritual that I have used for many years. The total time from beginning to end is 25 to 30 minutes.

6. Read the Bible and devotional materials. When I get up from the floor, I spend five or ten minutes reading from the Bible or other devotional and inspirational books. Shortly thereafter, I retire for a good night's sleep.

THE SECRET SEVEN

We all pick up nuggets of wisdom during our lives: some choice advice from a friend, a phrase from a sermon, a quote from a book, insight gained from a crisis in life. We all like to share these nuggets at times. Over the years I have done this and call them my Secret Seven. I would like to share them with you. The bits I offer help me to maintain good mental health and proper perspectives on life. Perhaps they will be of help to you in your Productive Prayer.

1. **Accentuate the positive.** Take time each day for yourself during which you think positively about yourself and muse about the good things in your life.

2. **Eliminate the negative.** Spend less time with hostile, negative persons who *add little* to your emotional well-being and *subtract much*.

3. **Fill your cup of good will.** Spend more time with gentle, positive persons who *add much* to your emotional well-being and *subtract little*.

4. **Do what you like.** Budget some time each week for "fun things" such as sports, hobbies, and activities that offer a change of pace and put you in complete control.

5. **It's OK for us to have a few warts.** Accept your own flaws and those of others as part of life.

6. **Collect people not things.** Try to maintain a well-rounded life that offers growth for mind, body, and spirit.

7. **Grant yourself wisdom and courage for the living of your days.** Enjoy the rich heritage of your church or synagogue and let more of its music and literature stir your soul and nourish your spirit.

YOU CAN BE CHANGED

One summer my family and I attended worship with a small congregation in the Bemidji-Cass Lake area in northern Minnesota. The sermon that Sunday, a dialog between the pastor and one of the elders, was entitled, "If God Could Speak." The pastor read the part of a man who was saying the Lord's Prayer, and the church elder, a retired college teacher with a beautiful deep voice, read the part of God.

As the Lord's Prayer was read in the dialog, the voice of God interrupted to ask questions, "How closely do you follow these requests?" "What do the words and phrases mean?" This dramatic method challenged the man who was automatically rattling off the words and forced him to re-think their true meaning. It reminded me of what C. S. Lewis said in *Screwtape Letters*, "Simply to say prayers is not to pray."

The sermon ended by forcibly bringing home to the man in the skit—on a point-by-point basis—the value of prayer. The voice of God concluded by saying, "Praying is a dangerous thing. You could wind up changed, you know!"

That, of course, is the point of spiritual growth. You could wind up changed. Changed in your perceptions —in your Christian perspectives. Changed in the way you deal with others. Changed in the way you handle stressful events.

Stress/Unstress is more than a book about how to handle stress. It is really a book about how to handle life. You are now ready to wrap everything up with your Personal Action Plan.

19

Your Personal Action Plan

You have now learned about the causes and casualties of stress (Part I—Understanding Stress) and its cure and control (Part II—Managing Stress) through applications of each of the Five Ways. You are now ready to put that information to work. You are now ready to draw up your Personal Action Plan.

But first, you need to know some background. You'll remember from Chapter 2 that part of Dr. Selye's Secret Recipe was choosing your life's goals. This chapter tells about such goal setting and planning. Experts in psychology and sociology have discovered that there are six major sectors that can be identified in the life of each of us: spiritual, family, financial/business/professional, physical, social, and mental. One method to visualize this is the concept of the Wheel of Life shown on the next page.

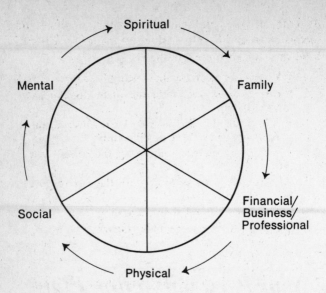

The priorities assigned to each sector vary from person to person. We all know people who devote a disproportionate amount of time to one sector at the expense of others: executives who spend nearly all their time and energy on company business (financial/business/professional) or persons who pursue, on a nearly full-time basis, the activities of country club and community events (social). Such one-sided individuals choose a certain sector and follow it with an intensity that children and spouse, physical health, religious or spiritual life, and other aspects can be left at the side of the road. This can lead to a variety of problems.

PRELIMINARY PLANNING

Before you develop your Personal Action Plan, let's assume there are some things you'd like to change.

As part of your preliminary planning, analyze the sectors in your life. On a sheet of paper reply with brief answers to these questions:

1. What pleases you most about your life so far?
2. What has been your most important accomplishment to date?
3. If you had your life to date to do over again, what would you want to do differently?
4. What do you *expect to do* during the rest of your life?
5. What would you *like to do* with the rest of your life (if different from 4)?
6. What is your purpose in life regarding:
   —being considered successful by others?
   —accumulating money?
   —achieving fame?
   —raising a healthy and happy family?
   —being a good member of your church or synagogue?

Now, on another sheet of paper, list everything you can think of that *makes you feel good.* (This method of goal setting and planning was developed in conjunction with Robert E. Griswold, president of Effective Learning Systems, Inc., in Edina, Minnesota.) Write down as many as possible now and then add others to the list for a few days. Here are some examples:

> *These things make me feel good:*
> —listening to George Gershwin music
> —taking a walk with my dog
> —reading poetry
> —camping with my kids
> —hiking in the outdoors with my spouse

Then, on another sheet of paper make a list of things you would *like to gain, possess, or accomplish* in your life. Here are some examples for your "wish list":

—I wish there was something I could do for my spiritual life. I'd like to go on a retreat to think about things for a week.

—Our son is growing up so fast. I would like to take him to Disneyland in the next year or so.

—I'd like to lose 30 lbs. in the next six months.

—I want to be involved with more work with artistic things; I'd better think of changing jobs.

—I wish I could become a good cross-country skier. I think the exercise would help me.

—I'd like to finish my college degree before my daughter graduates from high school.

—I wish we could get a bigger house so each of the children could have his own bedroom; then perhaps there wouldn't be so much arguing at home.

—I'd like to get a part-time job selling so I can learn some business skills.

—If we could get together enough money, I'd like to buy a small farm.

SETTING GOALS

Now, take six pieces of paper, one for each sector in the Wheel of Life:

1. On the top of each sheet write one of these sectors: Spiritual, Family, Financial/Business/Professional, Physical, Social, Mental.

2. Look at your "wish list" and sort it out according to the six sectors. If there are some sectors you aren't certain about, leave them blank for now. Put your "wishes" in the middle of each page.

Examples:
Spiritual
"Go on a church retreat."
"Talk to someone about my relationship with my daughter and her disinterest in church."

Family
"A bigger house."

Financial/Business/Professional
"Buy a small farm."

Physical
"Lose 30 lbs. in the next six months."

Social
(Leave blank if there are no goals from "wish list.")

Mental
"Finish my college degree."

3. Next, on the top of each of the six pages draw a line across the entire top of the page and number on a scale from 0 to 10 as shown below.

4. Now, in the most honest and objective way you can, put an X over the number on each line as to where you are *today*, in general. Then, if you had your way, where you would like to be on the scale in one year. Place an X with a circle around it there, as in the example. (Make sure these goals are *your goals* and not the goals of someone else such as parents, teacher, spouse, or friend!)

5. Now, on the bottom third of the page identify the probable benefits you could receive if you achieve the wish or goal you set for that sector and each of the other five sectors.

Examples of such benefits you might receive could include these examples:

   —"Make spouse feel happy."

   —"Enjoy my kids more."

   —"Make me feel better."

   —"Give me more freedom."

   —"Help me avoid death or premature illness."

—"Have money to go on a trip to Disneyland."
—"Bring me closer to God."

Here is an example of a typical worksheet:

Example: *Family*

X (where you are today) ⊗ (where you'd like to be in one year)

— X —————————————— ⊗ ————

0   5   10

Wish List
"I wish we could get a bigger house so that each of the children could have their own bedroom; then there wouldn't be so much arguing at home."

Probable Benefits
"Enjoy my kids more."
"Make spouse feel happy."
"Less stressful environment."

Barriers
"Even with my overtime work at the plant, mortgage money is so expensive."

6. Then, share your goals and probable benefits with someone you trust—and who will react to them in a positive, helpful way. Think about it for a few days and make sure *you* are comfortable with what you have written down on the bottom left of the page.

7. Now, with the help of this same person, try to identify *barriers* that can be seen in the pathway of achieving the goals you have set. List them on the bottom right. Examples of such obstacles might be:

—"I'm too busy with my five kids to take a class."
—"Even with my overtime work at the plant, mortgage money is so expensive!"
—"My dad would never let me do it."

Then think of ways of getting around the barriers. Finally, take a look at the X's on each sector line (where you are today) and place them in the corresponding positions on the Wheel of Life:

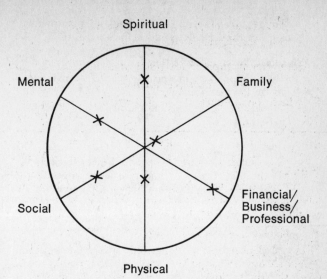

Spiritual

Mental

Family

Social

Financial/
Business/
Professional

Physical

PERSONAL ACTION PLAN

Here is how Tom L., a 52-year-old lawyer, completed his Wheel of Life and prepared his Personal Action Plan. Tom has been married to Sue for 25 years and is the father of two college-age daughters, Jane and Virginia. After going through the same process already outlined, he was ready to set his goals. Here are examples of his goals (his "wish list") for each sector:

Spiritual
- "I'd like to get over the 'spiritual letdown' I've had since my brother's death."
- "I need to feel more creative. How about singing in the choir?"

Family
- "I wish Sue and I could feel closer to each other. I thought we would be closer when the kids went to college, but it hasn't happened."

—"To get my sister-in-law to help us fix up our cabin at the lake. It would help her and us."

Financial/Business/Professional
—"Must supplement income because costs more to pay tuition than I planned."
—"Would like to get a young partner at my office to share the work."

Physical
—"Ever since my partner had his heart attack and left the firm, I've been under so much stress that I quit my jogging and don't have any energy any more."
—"Improve my sleep habits. I feel tired and irritable much of the time."

Social
—"Want to do more in neighborhood. Don't know anyone anymore."

Mental
—"I'd like to understand people better. Would like to take some psychology classes at our community college."
—"Should read more and watch less television."

He then plotted his findings (the rankings from 0 to 10) on the Wheel of Life. After Tom plotted his X's, he looked at where he is *today* (the dashed line) and saw a lopsided curve that seemed shallow in the Spiritual, Social, and Physical sectors. He mused, "Although I'm doing OK, I sure don't have a very 'well-rounded' life!"

As he thought of where he'd like to be in the future, he put the *circled* X's on the spokes of the Wheel. Much to his surprise, when he finished putting in where he thought he should be in a year and connected the points with a dotted line, the pattern was almost a circle—almost a well-rounded life.

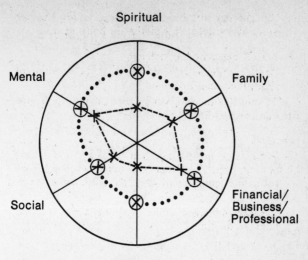

When Tom saw me a few weeks later, he showed me his Wheel of Life and his interest in developing a plan. After some discussions, we both agreed that the events related to his brother's death, his partner's resignation from the firm, and his relationship with his wife were causing more distress than he realized. I pointed out that stress was a significant factor in his fatigue, mild depression, insomnia, weight gain, and personal problems at home and the office.

As we talked about his situation, I discussed the Five Ways to Manage Stress and gave him many of the materials that appear in Part I and Part II of this book. As he left my office Tom told me he was determined to get in control of his life.

YOUR PERSONAL WELLNESS CONTRACT

I asked Tom several months later how he was doing. He said, "Everything has fallen into place, and once I finally started with the jogging, everything else became more doable. But," he concluded, "I had to talk myself into a contract!"

"A contract," I replied with surprise. "What do you mean by that?"

Tom continued, obviously pleased with himself, "After I finished my 'Wheel of Life' I read a good book by Dr. John Farquhar of Stanford, *The American Way of Life Need Not Be Hazardous to Your Health*. In it Dr. Farquhar described a Self-Contract."

I said, "That sounds like a great idea for a lawyer. Could you sue yourself for breach of contract?"

Tom answered quickly, "No, really, I know it sounds like a gimmick, but it worked for me. Here is what it looked like." He then handed it to me.

Personal Wellness Contract

I, _____, having completed
      (participant's name)
my Wheel of Life and Personal Action Plan, agree to use this Contract to improve my fitness level, control stress, and improve my general health status for the interval from:

    Start date: _____

    Finish date: _____

I realize that change is difficult, especially when changing long-established emotional habits regarding eating, exercise, and life-style. I also realize that practice and diligence will be required to polish the new skills I will learn. However, I now agree that I am ready to begin such change and am willing to affix my signature to this contract as evidence of my commitment.

Attached to this contract are the goals and Wheel of Life that I have studied and prepared.

Now with my concerted effort plus the help of God, my family, friends, and associates, I pledge to follow the attached Personal Action Plan.

_____   _____
(Participant signature)   (Address)

_____
(Date)

I looked it over and told Tom I liked his Personal Wellness Contract.

"If you want to use it in your book or classes you are free to use it," Tom said.

"No legal fees?" I queried with a smile.

"No charge whatsoever, on one condition," Tom answered. "If the user promises not to default on the contract!"

"Sounds like a good bargain to me," I concluded.

The Personal Wellness Contract you have signed is more than an attention grabber. It is even more than an indication that you have finished the book and agree to control stress more effectively—and creatively —and plan to follow through with a plan based on some well thought-out goals. The contract, in fact, should be considered a commitment to rethink your responsibility for the body, mind, and spirit that has been entrusted to you by God.

20

Unstress Places and Resources ·

The resource centers described in this chapter are places I have visited or learned about from reliable persons. Many of the books listed have been mentioned in *Stress/Unstress*. Others will help increase your knowledge about concepts related to stress management, nutrition, and exercise. I am indebted to Tom Ferguson, M.D., and his staff of *Medical Self-Care* for many of the brief annotations used in the listings of the books.

RESOURCE CENTERS

Center for the Well-Being of Health Professionals
200 Eastowne Drive, Suite 213
Chapel Hill, NC 27514
(919) 489-9167

Provides personal and professional help in promoting the physical and mental well-being of health workers and their families. Materials available for seminars, workshops, professional counselors, and treatment centers.

Center for Applied Behavioral Sciences
The Menninger Foundation
Box 829
Topeka, KS 66601
(913) 234-9566

The Center for Applied Behavioral Sciences is part of the Menninger Foundation, a renowned psychiatric, educational, and research facility. It provides seminars, workshops, consultation services, and educational materials for individuals, corporations, and human service agencies.

Tor Dahl & Associates
11 Lily Pond Road
St. Paul, MN 55110
(612) 483-4049

Presents two-day workshops and seminars designed to increase productivity through improved stress management and increased job satisfaction.

Effective Learning Systems
6950 France Avenue South
Suite 14
Edina, MN 55435
(612) 927-4171

Provides workshops on stress management for business organizations, governmental agencies, and the general public.

Executive Health Examiners
Psychological Services
777 Third Avenue
New York, NY 10017
(212) 486-8135

Offers individual stress check-up, biofeedback training, and Lunchtime Stress Talk seminars. Programs
implemented either on-site for corporations or at EHE
headquarters in New York.

Forbes Associates
477 Madison Avenue
New York, NY 10022
(212) 355-4540

Offers stress management programs designed for
business corporations. The Forbes staff does not provide clinical psychological services or individual
therapy. Theirs is an educationally oriented program
emphasizing prevention.

Georgetown Family Center
Department of Psychiatry
Georgetown University Medical Center
4380 MacArthur Boulevard, N.W.
Washington, DC 20007
(202) 625-7815

Conducts and provides a broad spectrum of sym-
posia, educational programs, and clinical services for
individuals, families, and professionals.

Learning for Health
1314 Westwood Boulevard
Suite 107
Los Angeles, CA 90024
(213) 474-6929

Provides a clinical program to help persons who are ill, overstressed, and those described as the "worried well."

The Levinson Institute, Inc.
Box 95
Cambridge, MA 02138
(617) 489-3040

Offers a wide variety of psychologic and psychiatric services to business corporations to help organizations and their employees adapt to stressful conditions and changing environments.

Pain and Health Rehabilitation Center
Route 2, Welch Coulee Road
LaCrosse, WI 54601
(608) 786-0611

Provides seminars for stress management and biofeedback training for professionals and interested lay persons. Also offers comprehensive 12-day program for chronic pain and stress control.

Stress Management Center of Metropolitan Washington
621 Maryland Avenue, N.E.
Washington, D.C. 20002
(202) 543-4945

Offers educational resources to lay public and professionals as individuals and in groups.

Whole Person Associates, Inc.
P.O. Box 3151
Duluth, MN 55803
(218) 728-4077

Provides continuing education seminars and consultations for human service professionals in a wide variety of health-care settings.

Wholistic Health Centers, Inc.
137 South Garfield
Hinsdale, IL 60521
(312) 323-1920

The Wholistic Health Centers in Hinsdale and Woodridge, Illinois, are church-based family practice medical care facilities that utilize an interdisciplinary team of physicians, pastoral counselors, and nurses who together focus on all aspects of an individual's health needs.

BOOKS

Antonovsky, Aaron. *Health, Stress and Coping*. San Francisco: Jossey-Bass Publishers, 1979. A rather technical but very exciting book that describes a kind of general field theory of health and disease. Antonovsky provides us with an underlying theme that makes it possible to consider, under one heading, all the kinds of things that explain a person's movement on the health/illness continuum.

Bailey, Covert. *Fit or Fat*. Boston: Houghton Mifflin Company, 1978. A readable, delightful introduction to the physiology of fat and the effects of exercise on fat and muscle. A useful tool for people who would like to start exercise programs but are afraid of biting off more than they can chew. Also recommended for those who have dropped out of too-strenuous exercise programs.

Bailey advises starting very gradually, just 12 to 20 minutes a day of step-ups, walking, or other aerobic activity, using your pulse as a guide to the appropriate exercise level.

Benowicz, Robert J. *Vitamins and You.* New York: Grosset and Dunlap, 1979. A useful, if somewhat rhetorical, overview, with an interesting analysis of the establishment stand on vitamin supplementation. Guidelines and advice on determining your own Optimal Personal Allowances for vitamins is innovative and helpful.

A special section gives a handy thumbnail summary of "the facts" on each vitamin, including U.S. Adult RDA, principal sources, antagonists/adversities/demands, synergistists/allies, normal functions, deficiency disorders, overdose, and exceptional needs.

Cooper, Kenneth H. *The Aerobics Way.* New York: Bantam Books, 1977. Cooper's first book, *Aerobics,* was based on his work with young and middle-aged Air Force men. This new book reflects his work with women, older people, and people with special medical problems, including obesity. There is a much more complete treatment of diet. More sports are included. There is a self-scoring coronary risk profile and an excellent bibliography.

Cousins, Norman. *Anatomy of an Illness as Perceived by the Patient.* New York: W. W. Norton, 1979. In 1964 Saturday Review editor Cousins was stricken with a severe debilitating illness. One of his doctors gave him one chance in 500 of recovery.

Determined to improve those odds, and with the cooperation and support of a wise and open-minded physician, he undertook some controversial intravenous Vitamin C treatments and an intensive course of laughter therapy—which included watching Marx brothers movies and "Candid Camera" reruns.

Cousins attributes his eventual recovery to his ability to trigger his body's own healing ability. He recounts his struggle step by step, taking a hard look at the medical care he received along the way. A final chapter recounts the experiences of some of the doctors and patients he has counseled since his recovery.

Downing, George. *The Massage Book*. New York: Random House, 1972. Probably the best available introductory book on massage. Excellent graphics show techniques in easy-to-do steps.

Dychtwald, Ken. *Bodymind*. New York: HBJ/Jove, 1977. The ways our feelings live in our bodies. A useful and important effort to synthesize the body wisdom underlying many seemingly different approaches—Rolfing, t'ai chi, yoga, encounter, massage, Feldenkrais exercises, gestalt therapy, etc.—to bodywork. Dychtwald pushes no particular approaches or theories and manages to avoid the air of righteousness sometimes encountered in books on body therapies.

Eisenberg, Arlene and Eisenberg, Howard. *Alive and Well: Decisions in Health*. New York: McGraw Hill Book Company, 1979. Although developed as a college text on health, this book would be suitable for your home bookshelf. Information is offered on preventive medicine, the patient-doctor partnership, and medical self-care. Excellent illustrations complement the text.

Farquhar, John W. *The American Way of Life Need Not Be Hazardous to Your Health*. New York: W. W. Norton and Co., 1978. Nearly all heart attacks and strokes are preventable. The behavioral risk factors are stress, poor diet, lack of exercise, overweight, and smoking.

Farquhar, director of the Stanford Heart Disease Prevention Program, starts out describing the elements of stress management. Developing unstressing skills can improve your ability to make changes in other areas. He goes on to explore exercise programs, eating sensibly without depriving yourself, losing weight, and quitting smoking.

Ferguson, Tom. *Medical Self-Care: Access to Health Tools*. New York: Summit Books, Simon & Schuster, 1980. This book is a compilation of articles that have appeared in *Medical Self-Care*, a quarterly magazine. There are a variety of reviews about the best of the popular medical books, articles about how lay persons can learn and practice basic paramedical skills, information about the way your life-style—eating, exercise, drugs, stress, and so on—affect your health. It also provides accounts of the growing self-care/self-help/health-consumer movement in America.

Fixx, James F. *The Complete Book of Running*. New York: Random House, 1977. This chatty, highly readable runner's gazetteer covers an amazing number of the big and little details—practical, physiological, philosophical—that take on increasing importance as running becomes an integral part of your life.

Friedman, Meyer and Rosenman, Ray H. *Type A Behavior and Your Heart*. Greenwich: Fawcett Books, 1974. The authors present evidence that speedy, impatient, highly-competitive people (mostly men) are at increased risk for heart disease, then tell you how to go about slowing down, becoming less competitive, learning patience. A landmark book. Especially important to men who find themselves trying to get ahead by constantly fighting time.

General Mills, Inc. *Family Health in an Era of Stress, 1978-79.* Minneapolis: General Mills, Inc., 1979. This useful 192-page book can be obtained without cost by writing to General Mills corporate headquarters, 9200 Wayzata Boulevard, Minneapolis, MN 55440.

Gerrard, Don. *One Bowl.* New York: Random House, 1974. This book is a daisy among the weedy stacks of diet books we receive each month. Gerrard has you choose a bowl with a special meaning for you and eat everything from that bowl—and to fill your bowl with only one thing at a time. He also suggests that in the beginning you eat alone, without distractions. Once you are free to give your full attention to eating, you can begin to focus on what your body really does want. Gerrard recommends you trust your urges.

Goldberg, Philip. *Executive Health.* New York: Mc-Graw Hill Paperbacks, 1978. An excellent guide to stress management in the corporate world.

Herbert, Victor. *Nutrition Cultism: Facts and Fiction.* Philadelphia: George F. Stickley Co., 1980. This excellent book written by the chief of the hematology and nutrition laboratory of the Bronx VA Medical Center gives 16 tips on how to spot food quacks. It offers useful information on nutrition, vitamins, and proper diet. The author provides background on organic food fallacy and legal recourse for victims of nutrition fraud.

Higdon, Hal. *Fitness Over Forty*. Mountain View, CA: Runners World, 1977. For this book, Higdon, a 45-year-old marathon runner, visited the best of the exercise gurus around the country. The result is a relaxed, readable, nondoctrinaire tour through a number of different exercise and diet regimens. It covers a variety of exercises too—biking, cross-country skiing, stationary running, racquetball, basketball, swimming, walking—with the most emphasis on running.

Jaffe, Dennis T. *Healing from Within*. New York: Alfred A. Knopf, Inc., 1980. In this practical guide, Dr. Jaffe shows how many common and potentially serious ailments can be affected by a holistic program which is developed in a coordinated effort between layman and professional. He emphasizes self-care techniques to mobilize the healing powers of the body and how pain and distress can be controlled without drugs. The book contains a wide range of ways to restore health and maintain it and provides an understanding of life's stresses and how they lead to disease.

Katch, Frank I., McArdle, William D., and Boyland, Brian Richard. *Getting in Shape: An Optimum Approach to Fitness and Weight Control*. Boston: Houghton Mifflin, 1977. The book on eating for people who run or want to run. Nutrition fundamentals are well illustrated and made relevant through continual reference to physical fitness. The sections on energetics, aerobics, and diet manage to simplify essential concepts without losing accuracy. The do-it-yourself calorie tables entertain.

Levin, Lowell, Katz, Alfred H., and Holst, Erik. *Self-Care: Lay Initiatives in Health*. New York: Prodist

Press, 1976. The report on a conference on self-care held in Copenhagen in 1976. Twenty-nine knowledgeable and articulate health planners spent several days brainstorming the possibilities and possible problems of an increasing emphasis on self-care. The book leaves little doubt that self-care will be part of our common health-care future. Contains the best available bibliography on self-care.

Maultsby, Maxie C. *Help Yourself to Happiness.* New York: Institute for Rational Living, 1976. This is the basic primer for rational self-counseling. It offers methods to achieve mental and emotional health.

McGinnis, Alan Loy. *The Friendship Factor.* Minneapolis: Augsburg Publishing House, 1979. This book offers "something extra" for people who want to get closer to the people they care for. It provides interesting insights into friendships between famous people, useful facts about human relationships, and tips on how to apply the insight in day-to-day situations.

Montagu, Ashley and Matson, Floyd. *The Human Connection.* New York: McGraw Hill Book Company, 1979. This book by anthropologist Montagu and social psychologist Matson explores the ways that we make connections with each other in approaching, touching, and communicating. They explore the world of the senses and communicative body motion. A landmark book in the field of human communication.

Pelletier, Kenneth R. *Mind as Healer, Mind as Slayer.* New York: Dell Publishing Company, 1977. The best available synthesis of our current understanding of stress as a cause of disease. Describes psychological factors that predispose one to illness and ways in which certain practices—meditations, biofeedback, relaxation—can be used as corrective measures.

A deep, thorough, and thoughtful examination of the ways that considerations of stress control can be a cornerstone of both self-care and professionally delivered health care.

Robertson, Laurel, Flinders, Carol, and Godfrey, Bronwen. *Laurel's Kitchen: A Handbook for Vegetarian Cookery and Nutrition*. New York: Bantam Books, 1976. The last 150 pages of this handsome vegetarian cookbook comprise the most intelligent and well-written popular introduction to nutrition to be found in local bookstores. This section, titled "Nutrition for a Meatless Diet," summarizes basic nutrition principles in an easily accessible manner.

Sehnert, Keith W. with Eisenberg, Howard. *How to Be Your Own Doctor (Sometimes)*. New York: Grosset and Dunlap, rev.ed. 1981. This book tells you how to go about becoming your own paramedic. It is one of the very best resources for anyone interested in self-care. The first 17 chapters of this book present the concept of the "activated patient," a layperson trained in basic clinical skills and capable of participating in the management of his or her own health care. The rest of the book—128 blue pages in the back—is the Medical Self-Care Guide. It gives detailed directions for dealing with the most common illnesses, accidents, and emergencies.

Selye, Hans. *The Stress of Life*. New York: McGraw Hill, 1976. A newly revised edition in which Selye describes his lifetime of research. It lets us read about the physiology of stress and learn about it as he did—discovery by discovery.

Shealy, C. Norman. *90 Days to Self-Health*. New York: The Dial Press, 1977. Dr. Shealy has put together a very practical and useful stress-reduction program for those who prefer exact directions to theory. His method is a simplified version of autogenic training (which makes extensive use of self-suggestion and visualization), with some additions, and brief practical recommendations on eating, exercising, and coping with pain.

Simonton, O. Carl, Mathews-Simonton, Stephanie, and Creighton, James. *Getting Well Again*. Los Angeles: J. P. Tarcher, Inc., 1978. Written by a physician and co-workers who believe that an individual's emotional experiences and attitudes have a direct bearing on the course of cancer therapy. In addition to providing the standard medical treatments, these clinicians attempt to influence their clients' attitudes and belief systems through teaching them visualization, relaxation skills, and new ways of dealing with resentment and anger.

Sobel, David S. *Ways of Health*. New York: Harcourt, Brace, Jovanovich, 1979. A fascinating, fairly academic anthology of writings in which Western-trained scientists examine the limits of contemporary Western medicine and take an open, yet critical look at ancient healing systems and some modern alternative health approaches.

Tubesing, Donald A. *Kicking Your Stress Habits*. Duluth: Whole Person Associates, 1980. This is a useful do-it-yourself guide to coping with stress. The author, psychologist and minister, views stress from a unique and pragmatic perspective developed through the institutional church and educational community.